Joan Sutherland & Richard Bonynge

with

THE AUSTRALIAN OPERA

by RICHARD BONYNGE

CRAFTSMAN HOUSE

To Moffatt Oxenbould,
with love and affection
and more thanks than I
can ever express

First published by Craftsman House,
Upper Level, 108 Pacific Highway,
Roseville, NSW 2069, Australia

Copyright © 1990, Richard Bonynge

ISBN 0 947131 37 X

Layout and Design: Rita Sarkis
Typesetter: Netan Pty Limited, Sydney
Printer: Tien Wah Press, Singapore

CONTENTS

Foreword

FOREWORD

J UST prior to Clara Butt's 1907 Australian tour, Nellie Melba offered her the following advice:

> 'So you're going to Australia?' she said. 'Well, I made twenty thousand pounds on my tour there but
> of course *that* will never be done again. Still, it's a wonderful country, and you'll have a good time.
> What are you going to sing? All I can say is — give 'em muck! It's all they can understand.'

Some eighty years have elapsed since Melba's advice to Clara Butt. The story appeared in Winifred Ponder's biography of the great English contralto, and when the book appeared in Australia after its publication in 1928, Melba vehemently (too vehemently?) denied the story and her lawyer forced the publishers to withdraw the offending passage from all unsold copies. Miss Ponder insisted that she had told the truth as Clara Butt had told it to her. But too late — the damage was done!

Could this possibly be the ancient cause of some Australian critics' preoccupation with the 'seriousness' of music? Nothing must be done for amusement or entertainment — only that which is deathly serious, or incomprehensible, can possibly be any good.

Having been educated in Australia, Joan and I have always been aware of these often loudly voiced sentiments. Having discovered abroad that there is indeed a great treasure chest of extraordinary music besides the well-loved classics we decided to bring some of it back to Australia, never mind the fuss.

We were happy and surprised to find our repertory well received by the public and the large majority of the critics. Of course the minority, who I'm sure would live ecstatically on a diet of Berg, Schoenberg and Stravinsky, were outraged and noisily so. But I think they are out of step with the times. All of the works we brought to Australia have been well received in Europe and America for the last two decades at least. And I think it not an exaggeration to say that the great part of the Australian public in understanding and enjoying them showed a sophistication equal to any audiences in London, Paris or New York.

I think this book will prove that in bringing 'our' operas to Australia we filled a gap in the repertoire while in no way overloading it in one direction or another.

No performer can perform alone. We are all at the mercy of our colleagues. In Australia we found such co-operation, such consideration and such friendliness as one does not find every day.

This book is not an autobiography but an attempt to put into perspective our operatic years in Australia beginning with the 1965 Sutherland-Williamson Season and continuing through our years with The Australian Opera. Nor does it pretend to be a history of The Australian Opera. I have concerned myself mostly with the works we performed both together and separately. As theatrical performances are ephemeral I feel some satisfaction in putting down these events for the record.

In order not to inflict too many opinions of my own on the reader I let the Australian press tell much of the story. Operatic doings receive fair space in Australian journalism, and, of course, at the hint of scandal the space doubles. As in the worlds of film, royalty or sport, opera stars receive their share of praise and abuse. If the one gives pleasure, the second must be endured. As they say, 'If you can't stand the heat, stay out of the kitchen'.

The Australian Opera is one of the last great opera companies left in the world. Covent Garden, the Metropolitan, the Paris Opera, San Francisco and Chicago no longer can be called true companies. Their performances are given mainly by guest artists who fly in and out and frequently rehearse minimally. Some of them have very short seasons.

Many Australians find it hard to believe that anything of a 'cultural' nature at home could possibly be on the high level that it must be overseas. My experience is that while standards in Europe and America have dropped appallingly, those in Australia have risen out of all proportion. The Australian Opera has a dedication, and a capacity for work second to none.

Joan and I would like so many of our colleagues to know how we have appreciated them, how we have enjoyed their company. If I err on the side of verbosity it is because I believe so many of their names belong in this book. As I have dealt with all the operas we performed I have tried to list the casts. I hope any unwitting omission will be forgiven — my memory is as faulty as the next person's.

But an opera company is made up of more than singers. The Elizabethan Sydney and the Elizabethan Melbourne orchestras gave me their solid best performances — I felt confident with them and we were able to make music together. Of course it is impossible to name all the members over the years, some of whom became good friends. Nevertheless, many come to mind.

Maurice Stead was the concert-master for the Sutherland-Williamson Season in 1965 and held the position with the Melbourne Orchestra for many years. In Sydney, Robert Ingram led the Orchestra when I first arrived and over the years the Orchestra has been led by Gordon Bennett, Brecon Carter, Peter Shaffer, Jan van der Berg, Ladislav Jasek, Vojtech Hlinka, Emil Kiss-Lazar, George Ermolenko and Wilfred Lehmann. All these gentlemen have my thanks in various ways for their expertise, their help and their friendliness.

So much of the success of a performance is due to the preparation beforehand, and here I have been fortunate over the years to have had much expert assistance. Many of my co-conductors also worked as *répétiteurs*, or as chorus masters — many of the *répétiteurs* worked as prompts or back-stage conductors. All of the following have helped in various ways to make The Australian Opera the fine company it is:

Peter Robinson, Stuart Challender, the late Peter Seymour, David Kram, Russell Channell, William Reid, the late Geoffrey Arnold, Martin Handley, Gordon Kember, Roland Peelman, David Stanhope, Torben Petersen, Peter Bandy, Julia de Plater, Simone Young, the late Gary Laycock, Michael Schouten, Narelle French, Caroline Lill (who was my right hand in the 1965 season) and last, but not least, Sharolyn Kimmorley who is now Head of Music Staff.

Many vocal experts from overseas came to work with our singers, bringing with them the highest standards. Anthony Legge, the late Jack Metz, Susan Webb, Miguel Pinto, Beatrice Webster and Michael Parker were and are greatly appreciated by the company.

On the production side I worked with Stuart Maunder, Michael Beauchamp, Tessa Bremner, Ruth Yeatman, Stephen Philips, Elke Neidhardt, Bryan Barnes, Peter Reeve, Ann Hoban, Anna Pappas, Tanya Leach, Nick Schlieper, Brad Jarrett, Ruth Catlin, Brian Fitzgerald, David Crooks, John Wregg, Michael Kaempff, Peter Jukes and Luise Napier. These, and many more who are mentioned in the text, and probably some I have omitted, all made working for The Australian Opera a happy experience.

In the library, Judith Jacks and Peter Alexander spent untold hours preparing and correcting orchestral parts. Renee Goossens and Marie-Claire have produced splendid results with French language, which is so difficult for us Anglo-Saxons! Choreographers Guillermo Keys-Arenas, Peter Bishop, Robert Ray, Lois Strike, Ian Castenetto, Carole Todd and Jak Callick did wonderful work with the ballet and some of the operas contained very substantial dancing.

Roger Barratt, Tony Everingham, Nigel Levings and Donn Byrnes were responsible for lighting so many of our shows — and so well.

In the office management and publicity department there have been so many who have gone out of their way to make life easier for Joan and myself. Cleo Caladoukas, Wendy Hill, Russell Mitchell, Judith Kolecany, Carole McPhee, David Colville, Josephine Ridge, Heather Grant, Joanne Graham, Bernard Davies, Mark Wheeler, Yvonne Schwerdt, Peter Bloor, Cheryl Forrest-Smith and Carmel Dalco — these are just the people we came into contact with from day to day.

In the workshops where the magnificent scenery is made and the beautiful costumes — a special thankyou to Bill Paterson who made so many of Joan's lovely clothes.

And then the days of performance … we saw the same faces backstage: the dressers, the wig department, the orchestra porters. We really miss them when we go away. The late Marge Helmore, Michael Beachey, Gabrielle Blackstock, Sandy Windon (who dressed Joan in so many operas), John Lauder (who created such beautiful makeup for her) and of course our darling Shirley Germain, who has attended to the wigs ever since we have been with The Australian Opera and who always spoilt us to death with constant cups of very weak tea throughout all our performances.

All these, and more, deserve and have very grateful thanks from Joan and myself — not only for their service to The Australian Opera but for their many kindnesses to ourselves.

Richard Bonynge

1

NINETEEN SIXTY FIVE

Although this book deals primarily with our association with The Australian Opera, I begin with a résumé of our 1965 season because it was to have such an effect on that Company.

Facing Page: Lucia di Lammermoor Act 2 Scene. 1

The firm of J.C. Williamson was the leading entrepreneurial organisation in Australia from the late 1880s, all but monopolising the Australian theatrical scene until well past the middle of this century. Williamson, an American actor, formed the Company and after his death it was run for many decades by the four brothers Tait.

In 1911, 1924 and 1928 the Tait brothers presented three Melba-Williamson seasons of opera in Australia. They were extremely adventurous in their repertoire and gave the first Australian performances of *Otello, Cavalleria Rusticana, Pagliacci, L'Amico Fritz, Fedora, La Gioconda, Madama Butterfly, Tosca, Il Trittico, Turandot* and *Thaïs*.

By the time we came to deal with 'The Firm' (as it was generally called), only the youngest brother, Sir Frank Tait — then in his eighties — was still alive. He told us that he had begun his career with Melba's last great season in Australia and he wanted to end it with a Sutherland tour. He made it possible for us to return to our country after an absence of fifteen years on my part and fourteen on Joan's. Together we formed the Sutherland-Williamson International Grand Opera Company which would tour the eastern Australian State capitals (Melbourne, Adelaide, Sydney and Brisbane) for fourteen weeks, playing eight times a week — matinees Wednesday and Saturday. This was certainly the last of the old-fashioned touring opera companies, never to be repeated because of the ever increasing demands of the unions, allied to general financial inflation.

The musical climate in Australia during the forties and fifties was a non-operatic one. There was almost no opera during the war and since then there had been three Italian tours of a fairly provincial standard, although with some good singers of whom I remember Rina Malatrasi, Dora Minarchi, Mercedes Fortunati and Alvinio Misciano. In Sydney in 1965, the only professional opera was run by the Australian Elizabethan Theatre Trust. Although this was a serious Company and would develop into The Australian Opera, it functioned on a shoe-string and played in a tiny, ugly theatre in what was then one of the worst slum districts of Sydney.

Sir Frank made a deal with this organisation that they would undertake the making of some of the sets and provide certain technical assistance, also that they would

Above: Lucia curtain call, Melbourne. On Joan's right, Norman Ayrton, Cornelis Opthof, Tonina Dorati, Clifford Grant, André Montal and Sergei Baigildin. On her left: John Alexander, Richard Bonynge and Dorothy Cole

pay half the losses incurred by the season. This latter agreement seemed a very smart move on Sir Frank's part but, in fact, the deficit was minimal and they ended up only paying thirteen thousand pounds each. Reading today of the hundreds of thousands and even millions of deficit incurred by some opera companies, this now seems absurd! J.C. Williamson's begged us to prolong the tour for another two or three weeks which would have taken care of the deficit but, although we would have loved to oblige, we (and others in the Company) had previous commitments.

With his knowledge and long experience of Australian theatre audiences, Sir Frank wanted us to play *La Bohème, Madama Butterfly* and *La Tosca* on the evenings when Joan was not singing. I was young and inexperienced enough to be idealistic and wanted to show a repertoire to Australia that was less familiar and, I believed, more interesting. Of course, there would probably have been no deficit if I had listened to Sir Frank but then Australia would have been the poorer, operatically speaking. I liked and admired Sir Frank very much indeed but I was very headstrong. We argued by the hour about every penny — J.C. Williamson's expected the best at bargain prices!

As Artistic Director I was eventually given carte-blanche to engage and cast the singers and choose the operas. My first thought, naturally, was to create a great ambience for Joan's return home but I also wanted this to be the best Company that Australia had ever seen. The great catch was that Sir Frank was very canny with the money so that 'carte-blanche' was merely a manner of speaking. He wanted me to engage Italians, feeling that the Australian public still clung to the belief that Italians were the best singers. I wanted to engage singers whom I knew were dependable — singers with star voices, dramatic ability, looks and allure. We ended up with one of the handsomest companies ever assembled, vocally and histrionically.

Australian audiences (like most) love tenors and we tried not to disappoint. It was fortunate that I had heard early in 1963 a young Italian just at the beginning of his career — Luciano Pavarotti was the first to be signed and his contract

Above: La Sonnambula Act 3.
Taken in the dressing room
Left: La Sonnambula Act 1

stipulated three performances a week from his repertoire of Edgardo in *Lucia di Lammermoor*, Alfredo in *La Traviata*, Elvino in *La Sonnambula* and Nemorino in *L'Elisir d'Amore*. He sang every one of his scheduled performances, as did almost every member of the Company. The schedule was never changed and only in two or three minor cases was the cast altered at the last moment. The other star tenor was John Alexander of the Metropolitan Opera. I had conducted *Faust* with him in Vancouver where he also sang Pollione to Joan's first *Norma*. His acceptance boded well for the tenor wing — he sang Edgardo, Alfredo, Faust, and Lenski in *Eugene Onegin*. Our third tenor was Alberto Remedios from Sadler's Wells, engaged for Edgardo, Faust, Lenski and Alfredo. He was joined by Joseph Ward from Covent Garden (to sing Idreno in *Semiramide*, Elvino, Nemorino, Gaston in *Traviata* and M. Triquet in *Onegin*) and André Montal, a young American, for performances of Idreno, Elvino, Arturo, Gaston and M. Triquet.

In engaging the sopranos, I had to find singers who were capable of singing Joan's roles. There were to be seven operas in the repertoire — five of these contained

Above: La Sonnambula Act 3
Sleepwalking Scene
Right: La Sonnambula Act 1 with Joseph
Rouleau as the Count

Above: The last night of the season in Melbourne with the Company on stage at the final curtain calls, *La Sonnambula*
Left: Singing 'Home, Sweet Home' on the last night of the Melbourne Season. Immediately behind Joan is Adelio Zagonara, our prompter from La Scala, and on her right are Ronald Maconaghie, Doris Yarick, Richard Cross and Spiro Malas.

Joan's star roles: Lucia, Amina in *La Sonnambula*, Violetta in *La Traviata*, Marguerite in *Faust*, and *Semiramide*. *L'Elisir d'Amore* was an obvious vehicle for Pavarotti and *Eugene Onegin* was included as a good company opera and a contrast to the *bel canto* works. All operas were to be performed in the original language, except *Eugene Onegin*, which was sung in English.

Elizabeth Harwood, the beautiful English soprano, was then at the beginning of her career and she joined us to sing Lucia, Amina, and Adina in *L'Elisir d'Amore*, as well as singing Lisa in *La Sonnambula* on the nights that Joan sang Amina. Doris Yarick, who had sung Marguerite in *Faust* with me in Vancouver and also Susanna in *The Marriage of Figaro*, sang Marguerite, as well as Tatiana in *Eugene Onegin*, Lisa in *La Sonnambula* and Giannetta in *L'Elisir d'Amore*, and showed her company spirit by taking the almost non-existent part of the Princess Azema in *Semiramide*. Queenslander Margreta Elkins had been singing as a mezzo-soprano but was unhappy in that register and was at the time flirting with the soprano range. She sang

Above Top: (Left to right) John
Alexander (Lensky), Richard Cross
(Onegin), Margreta Elkins (Tatiana),
Lauris Elms (Olga) rehearsing second
act of *Eugene Onegin*
Above: La Traviata Act 3.
(Right to left) Luciano Pavarotti,
Cornelis Opthof, Spiro Malas, Joseph
Ward, Monica Sinclair, Joan
Sutherland, Ronald Maconaghie,
Clifford Grant

Adina, Tatiana, and Siebel in *Faust*. One other Australian, Joy Mammen, sang
Violetta, Tatiana, Lisa and Giannetta.

The entire Company proved very co-operative in singing the smaller roles — the
only exceptions being those who sang three major performances in a week. I am very
much a believer in the adage that there are no small parts, only small singers, and it
was heartening to see artists taking just as much care and trouble with tiny roles as
with star parts, thus strengthening performance standards.

For mezzo-sopranos we had Covent Garden's Monica Sinclair, the Australian
Lauris Elms who had also been singing at Covent Garden, the American Dorothy
Cole and the Scot Morag Beaton. Monica and Lauris shared the difficult part of
Arsace in *Semiramide*, also Olga in *Eugene Onegin* and Martha in *Faust*, whilst in

Above: *La Traviata* Morag Beaton
as Annina
Left: *La Traviata* Act 3 with Spiro
Malas, as the Baron

Traviata Monica sang Flora, and Lauris — Annina. Morag Beaton sang Larina
(*Onegin*), Teresa (*Sonnambula*), Annina, Alisa, Siebel and one performance of
Tatiana. Dorothy Cole was Larina, Teresa, Flora, Alisa and Martha.

The baritones were the Dutch-Canadian Cornelis Opthof, Robert Allman and
Ronald Maconaghie — both Australian. Opthof sang Enrico (*Lucia*), Germont
(*Traviata*), Belcore (*L'Elisir*) and Valentin (*Faust*), Allman the same four roles as
well as Onegin, and Maconaghie sang Belcore, the Marquis in *La Traviata*, Oroe in
Semiramide and Zaretsky in *Onegin*.

The four basses were the French-Canadian Joseph Rouleau, two Americans —
Spiro Malas and Richard Cross — and the Australian, Clifford Grant. Rouleau sang
Raimondo in *Lucia*, Dulcamara in *L'Elisir*, Prince Gremin in *Onegin*, Assur in

Semiramide, Mephistopheles in *Faust* and Count Rodolfo in *La Sonnambula*. Cross
sang Raimondo, Assur, Gremin, Mephistopheles, and the Baron in *Traviata*. Malas
sang Dulcamara, Assur, Gremin, Rodolfo and the Baron, and Grant — Raimondo,
Gremin, the Doctor in *Traviata* and the Ghost in *Semiramide*.

The year before the tour I flew to Melbourne and listened to one hundred and fifty
singers in order to choose the chorus of thirty-six. And what a chorus! They were
one of the glories of the season. Some of them went on to have important solo
careers while many of them are still in the opera world twenty-plus years later.
Donald Shanks became a leading bass with The Australian Opera (he sometimes
sang the Doctor in our *Traviatas*). Tom McDonnell has had a long career with
English National Opera (he sang Alessio in *La Sonnambula*). Sergei Baigildin (who
sang Normanno in *Lucia* and one Lenski) and Mary Hayman (who appeared as
Giannetta in *L'Elisir d'Amore*) became principals with The Australian Opera. Judith
Turner joined Sadler's Wells where she sang such roles as Santuzza and Brünhilde.
John Heffernan (now John Aron) is currently in the London production of
Phantom of the Opera. Other stalwarts of the chorus were Elizabeth Allen, who sang
Filipyevna in *Eugene Onegin*, Josephine Bermingham, Betty Greenfield (who
appeared as Larina), Chesne Ryman who continues her career in Sweden, and John
Durham, who retired from The Australian Opera in 1988 along with Elizabeth
Allen and Josephine Bermingham in 1988-9. From the ballet, Judy Hoskins married
Alberto Remedios and Alex Burns became Wardrobe Director for The Australian
Opera.

The beginning of the tour was very demanding. The whole Company was
together for only three complete weeks before opening night in Melbourne at Her
Majesty's Theatre. We played three operas in the first week — *Lucia, Onegin* and

Above Top: L'Elisir d'Amore Spiro Malas as Dulcamara with Luciano Pavarotti as Nemorino

Above: L'Elisir d'Amore Spiro Malas (Dulcamara) with Elizabeth Harwood (Adina)

Right: Joan Sutherland as Marguerite in *Faust* (The Garden Scene)

Traviata — and added one opera per week so that by the end of the Melbourne season the repertoire was complete.

I had asked the British director, Norman Ayrton, to come with us and he undertook the mammoth task of directing five of the operas. But more than this, he organised the entire rehearsal schedule in an extraordinarily efficient manner. To his firm hand and co-ordinating ability the season owed much of its success. The other two operas (*Sonnambula* and *L'Elisir*) were directed by Martin Scheepers, a fine dancer from the Royal Dutch Ballet, and later American Ballet Theatre, who also did the choreography for all operas, and danced as well. As we played the whole of the ballet in *Faust* this was no mean achievement.

As assistant conductors we had Gerald Krug and Georg Tintner, both from the Elizabethan Theatre Trust Opera, and William Weibel from the Metropolitan Opera. They also worked with the chorus and as *répétiteurs*, in which latter task they were joined by Caroline Lill who later became one of the backbones of The Australian Opera music staff and by Brian Stanborough and Gwen Halstead. I generally conducted four times a week and did not miss attending any of the one hundred and twenty performances.

As for Joan, she sang some of the best performances of her career, twelve *Violettas*, eleven *Lucias*, eight *Semiramides*, six *Aminas* and six *Marguerites*. Her stamina was amazing. At the beginning of the tour she sang the dress rehearsal of *La Sonnambula* one morning (in full voice, remembers Pavarotti) and *La Traviata* the same night. Of course, many of the other singers sang just as much but she felt the responsibility of the season on her shoulders and the receptions and interviews were endless. The entire Company rehearsed unsparingly in a gruelling schedule — but no one complained. There was very little back-biting and the spirit of the whole ensemble was magnificent. We coped as well as we could but became somewhat frayed at times and had quite a 'to do' with the press in Sydney, all of which has been written about elsewhere. Of course, it is very funny twenty or so years later, but at the time we were just tired out and our sense of humour was momentarily dormant!

The opening night in Melbourne was a very great thrill and a complete public and critical success, but the night I will remember to my grave is the final one in Melbourne — a performance of *La Sonnambula*. After applauding for some forty

Above Top: Semiramide Act 2. Joseph Ward as Idreno and Doris Yarick as Azema. The three ladies on the left are Mary Hayman, Betty Greenfield and Judy Duggan
Above: Semiramide. Joan wore her nineteenth-century Spanish garnet earrings with this costume

Above: In the dressing room with hair-do for *Semiramide*
Right: Joan Sutherland as Semiramide, Monica Sinclair as Arsace, and Joseph Rouleau as Assur

minutes (with the complete Company on stage in formal dress as well as those who had taken part that night) the audience began chanting 'Home, Sweet Home', over and over. From somewhere backstage an awful upright piano appeared and I accompanied Joan as she sang the old song. The theatre was full of love that night. I don't know who thought to bring in the piano, but the whole thing just happened and no-one can ever take away the joy of that evening from us.

The Age reported:

> 'Flowers and streamers blanketed the stage, women in evening gowns stood on seats and applause continued for forty minutes.'

and *The Melbourne Herald:*

> 'The effect was magical, and I doubt whether anything like it has ever been seen in Australia before.'

There were amusing incidents along the way. A certain singer got very, very drunk (for an emotional reason, not habitual) and was brought to the theatre quite incapable of dressing himself, let alone making up. Friends in the chorus did this for him and shoved him onto the stage for his entrance. He promptly swayed straight across and out the other side. He was helped back on again and more or less pushed around all evening. The extraordinary thing was that he sang his most accurate performance of the season.

On another night a baritone (while quite sober) suddenly went completely blank at the entrance of Germont in the third act of *La Traviata*. There was an enormous pause. The prompt, who was dear old Adelio Zagonara, the famous comprimario from La Scala, was practically jumping out of the prompt box in agitation and just as Luciano thought he might as well sing the line for him our friend bellowed forth stentorially, 'Cortigiani'! Monica Sinclair collapsed into very audible and hysterical giggles, along with most of the cast, and I must confess it was rather difficult to continue. Unfortunately he had his Verdi roles momentarily confused and had sung a line with almost identical notes from *Rigoletto* instead! The singer in question hotly denies the story to this day — as I like him immensely I will spare his blushes. However, Luciano, Joan, Monica and myself all swear the story is true!

In these days when new artists burst onto the scene like comets, are acclaimed as stars and vanish in a few years, it is more than interesting to trace what has become of this group which formed the Sutherland-Williamson Company. Elizabeth Harwood became a popular European star and worked a great deal with von Karajan. Margreta Elkins continues her long and honourable career in concerts, and — having announced her operatic retirement only two years ago — like Melba, has reconsidered, and is back on the stage! Doris Yarick is now head of the opera department at Yale University and Joy Mammen is a leading teacher at London's Royal Academy of Music. Monica Sinclair added to her many recording commitments and sang a great deal in Europe. She is now mainly teaching. Morag Beaton had major successes with The Australian Opera as Turandot, Venus in *Tannhauser* and other dramatic soprano roles. Dorothy Cole married and retired from the stage.

Luciano Pavarotti made an enormous career — we worked most recently in 1988 in *Il Trovatore* at the Metropolitan Opera. John Alexander is currently engaged by the Metropolitan where he has sung for almost thirty years. Alberto Remedios

Above: Semiramide singing the aria 'Bel raggio ...'

Above: Relaxing during the tour: Martin Scheepers, Margreta Elkins, Joy Mammen and Richard Bonynge
Right: (Left to right) Gerald Krug, Joan Sutherland, Morag Beaton, Richard Bonynge and André Montal photographed at Point Piper where we stayed during the Sydney visit

developed into a fine Wagnerian tenor and continues his career in splendid voice. Joseph Ward is Head of Vocal Studies at the Royal Northern College of Music, and André Montal occupies the same position in the University of Kentucky, after having spent some years singing in Germany. Cornelis Opthof performed the part of Michonnet in *Adriana Lecouvreur* with us in Toronto as recently as 1987, and has a busy career.

Robert Allman is a leading baritone with The Australian Opera. Joseph Rouleau is still singing internationally, and Spiro Malas is on contract to the Metropolitan Opera. Richard Cross, after a long career at the Frankfurt Opera, only recently retired to teach, and Clifford Grant whose career became international is still with The Australian Opera, although threatening to retire to paint and fish!

Norman Ayrton was Director of the London Academy of Music and Dramatic Art for many years and then went to the Juilliard School in New York, where he headed their opera department for some ten years. Meanwhile he directed for Covent Garden, The Australian Opera and various American companies. Recently he has been Director of Opera at London's Royal Academy of Music. Martin Scheepers died tragically in 1986.

The designing of the entire sets and costumes was put into the hands of Tonina Dorati. This was an impossible task for any one person at all, let alone a very young and relatively inexperienced girl. She was chic and charming and the daughter of the late Hungarian conductor, Antal Dorati. Her costumes were magnificent and her sets always adequate and in some instances very good. But in the time allowed, the bulk of the work was overwhelming. She completed all the costumes and five of the sets on schedule, leaving *La Sonnambula* and *Semiramide* in a rather sketchy state. I showed her a set of designs for *Sonnambula* which our late friend, the painter Roy Hobdell, had designed for Covent Garden, and she cleverly and quickly adapted these. As for *Semiramide*, Norman Ayrton and some of the technical staff put together old *Aida* sets with lots of drapes and some added Babylonian motifs. It all worked and many people remember it as being quite handsome — distance

Left: (Left to right) Suzie Alexander, Elizabeth Harwood, John Alexander, Norman Ayrton, Joseph Rouleau, Luciano Pavarotti, Marlena Malas, William Weibel, Spiro Malas, Alberto and Judy Remedios, and kneeling, Clifford Grant

undoubtedly lending enchantment! Originally Henry Bardon had been invited to design, but his then extremely modest fees were refused by J.C. Williamson's and I would be ashamed to say how little Tonina was paid. She survived, and became a most successful fashion designer.

Moffatt Oxenbould, who was very young at the time, was one of our stage managers (along with Peter Smith and Bob Herbert). He looked even younger and was more than once taken for our son standing in the wings, although there is no physical resemblance whatever. I know he is the first to admit that this exposure to so many great singers gave him a solid background for his many years with The Australian Opera as Artistic Administrator and I think he has earned his current post of Artistic Director with the Company.

2

NINETEEN SEVENTY FOUR

The Australian Opera, formerly the Elizabethan Trust Opera Company, was inaugurated in 1970 and moved into the newly completed and much publicised Sydney Opera House in 1973. We had been invited to open the theatre but because of strikes and various delays the opening date was changed more than once and our commitments precluded our acceptance. So our first appearance in the house and with the Company took place in 1974 with *Les Contes d'Hoffmann*. Our contract was first mooted when Donald McDonald was General Manager but, in one of the myriad shakeups in Australian Opera administration, this position on our arrival was held by a Danish musician and pianist, John Winther.

For our second return home we were treated to a superb production designed by Jose Varona and directed by Tito Capobianco. The cast was a fine one — the Mauritian-Australian tenor, Henri Wilden, in the title role, Raymond Myers in the four baritone roles, and Huguette Tourangeau, the Canadian mezzo-soprano, as the Muse and Nicklausse. Graeme Ewer played Andrès, Cochenille, Pitichinaccio and Frantz, and Elizabeth Connell (who now sings major soprano roles all over the world) was the voice of Antonia's mother. The two students in the Prologue were played by John Pringle and Anson Austin, both to become leading singers with The Australian Opera. Donald Solomon was Luther, Robert Eddie — Schlemil, grant Dickson — Crespel, and Ronald Maconaghie — Spalanzani. All these singers were new to us with the exception of Huguette, who had performed the same role with us at the Metropolitan Opera earlier in the same year, Raymond Myers with whom we had performed *The Messiah* in The Royal Festival Hall, London, in 1967, and Ron Maconaghie from our 1965 season.

'Dazzling', said the nationalistic *National Times* ... 'even in French'.

Maria Prerauer wrote:

'Saturday's opening was so sensational that the world should beat a path to Bennelong Point just to see it — only you can't get a ticket for love nor money.'

'Fans offer $500 for Sutherland opera seats',

proclaimed *The Sun-Herald*.

Facing Page: Les Contes d'Hoffmann as Antonia with Raymond Myers as Dr Miracle. (His wig leaves much to be desired!)

Above: Olympia in *Les Contes
d'Hoffmann*
Right: Les Contes d'Hoffmann Giulietta
with Henri Wilden as Hoffmann

Above: Curtain call in the Stella costume after *Les Contes d'Hoffmann*

W.L. Hoffmann in *The Canberra Times:*

> 'A triumph, one of those rare occasions that will forever be remembered in the history of opera in this country ... the finest The Australian Opera has yet achieved.'

Felix Werder in *The Age* had his own point of view:

> 'This was another of those low-brow rejects from Vaudeville which The Australian Opera keeps on keeping on.'

Australians obviously liked the low-brow reject — they flew in from all over the country and paid high prices for black-market tickets.

At the end of the first evening the General Manager announced that we had accepted appointments as honorary life members of the Company. Roger Covell commented in *The Sydney Morning Herald:*

> '(This) might be taken as a pleasant but empty gesture. I believe it is much more than that. It signifies the visitors' full acceptance of The Australian Opera as a Company to which they will gladly return.'

The opera was broadcast by the Australian Broadcasting Commission and we gave eight performances between 13 July and 6 August. Just before the run we gave two recitals in the Opera House, and afterwards, two more in Dallas Brooks Hall, Melbourne — a big mish-mash of a programme with songs by Dalayrac, Haydn, Meyerbeer, David, Rossini, Donizetti, Benedict, Gretchaninov, Cui, Reger, Abt, Ponchielli, Delibes, Bizet, Chaminade and Offenbach!

This was to be our shortest season in Australia for many a year. Before we returned to Europe John Winther asked me to become Musical Director of The Australian Opera. I accepted, having no idea of the work I was letting myself in for, not to mention the fights and frustrations. It was one of the better decisions I made in my life and it brought me great joy — I've always enjoyed a good fight!

3

NINETEEN SEVENTY SIX

The generous Federal grant to The Australian Opera between 1974 and 1976 by the Government (under Gough Whitlam, the Labor Prime Minister profoundly interested in the Arts) plummeted disastrously when the Liberal Party come to power in 1975. Since the opening of the Sydney Opera House in 1973 the Company had been able to budget luxuriously, experimenting with esoteric repertoire. Suddenly everything changed. Ticket prices went up and the Board's message was 'economise' and 'play more performances'. The Company was stretched to an unhealthy limit in order to increase returns at the box office.

Facing Page: Lakmé Act 1

In 1975 there had been 194 performances, but in 1976 this was increased to 269 — small wonder that singers were constantly cancelling because of illness. Many thought this distressing situation was caused by the air-conditioning at the Opera House — an almost hermetically sealed building — where it was generally imagined by the singers that the air was changed once a week. Possibly, but the cruel workload of the chorus, orchestra and many principals was disastrous.

As Musical Director I had little to say in the general running, business-wise, of the Company. My job was to choose the repertoire, cast the operas, rehearse and conduct — and enough too. I was content working with John Winther whose opinions deserved respect, and I am eternally grateful to Moffatt Oxenbould who was such a help to me in innumerable ways. He knew every member of the Company and cared about them. He was a workaholic who frequently made himself ill by doing too much. Without him I wouldn't have lasted two seasons. He knew how to reason me out of my wilder excesses; his suggestions were often more than helpful and he took the load of clerical work off my shoulders.

My first thought was the repertoire which I began to draw up in 1974, although even then much of 1976 was already contracted. Both John Winther and the previous Musical Director (Edward Downes) favoured the modern school and since the formation of The Australian Opera in 1970 the repertoire included *Les Noces* and *The Rake's Progress* (Stravinsky), *Mahagonny* (Weill), *War and Peace* (Prokofiev), *Jenufa* and *The Cunning Little Vixen* (Janacek), *The Rape of Lucretia*, and *Albert Herring* (Britten), *Wozzeck* (Berg), *Salome*, *Ariadne* and *Der Rosenkavalier* (Richard Strauss), and four Australian operas: *The Affair* (Felix Werder), *Lenz* (Larry Sitzky), *Rites of Passage* (Peter Sculthorpe), and *Hero* (Craig McGregor).

Many of these operas would continue to be performed but it was necessary to restore a more moderate balance. There was no serious *bel canto*, practically no

French opera, and no eighteenth century opera apart from Mozart. There were the popular Verdi and Puccini, three Wagner and several Gilbert and Sullivan's. Now, with less money to play with, the Board constantly exhorted us to fill the houses.

The 1976 Annual Report tells that, of the operas played between 1972 and 1976, *Wozzeck* played to 59.8 per cent capacity, *Albert Herring* 47.9 per cent, *Les Noces* with *L'Amfiparnasso* (Vecchi) 35.7 per cent, *Lenz* and *The Affair* 26.4 per cent and *Hero* 11 per cent, causing enormous losses for the Company. On the other hand, *The Magic Flute, Don Giovanni, Aida, Nabucco, L' Elisir d'Amore, Carmen* and *Lakmé* all played to over 90 per cent of capacity.

Twenty-four operas were performed during the 1976 season: new productions of *The Abduction from the Seraglio, Wozzeck* (for the Adelaide Festival), *Hero, The Cunning Little Vixen, Lakmé, Carmen* and a double-bill of *Les Noces* and *L'Amfiparnasso* in association with the Sydney Dance Company — and revivals of *Aida, Salome, The Magic Flute, Albert Herring, Così fan tutte, Der Rosenkavalier, Simon Boccanegra, The Barber of Seville, A Masked Ball, Rigoletto, The Marriage of Figaro, Jenufa, La Boheme, H.M.S. Pinafore* and *Iolanthe.*

I made my début as Musical Director during the Summer Season (January-February) in the revival of John Copley's production of *The Magic Flute*, an opera I could happily conduct every week of my life. The cast included Anson Austin as Tamino, Dolores Cambridge, Mary Hayman and Angela Giblin as the Three Ladies, John Pringle as Papageno, Rhonda Bruce as the Queen of the Night, Isobel Buchanan as Pamina, Graeme Ewer as Monostatos, Grant Dickson as the Speaker, Donald Shanks as Sarastro, Neville Grave and John Germain as the Priests, Cynthia Johnston as Papagena, Lamberto Furlan and Joseph Grunfelder as The Armed Men. We gave six performances, of which I conducted the first three.

Brian Hoad in *The Bulletin:*

> 'An auspicious sort of début for a musical director. Bonynge's light and lively approach … restores to these guardians of enlightenment the warm glow of humanity which is right-fully theirs.'

> 'A Mozartian conductor of authentic flair',

said Roger Covell in *The Sydney Morning Herald*, where he wrote of the new Pamina (making her début with the Company):

> 'Miss Buchanan has a voice that registers with exceptional definition, even when she is using it as softly as possible. It has formidable reserves of power and fullness … Mr Bonynge, whose protégé she is, must have been heartened by her vindication of his faith, judgement and guidance …'

I was heartened indeed. Isobel had sung for me in London straight from music school and I was deeply impressed by her rich and already mature voice, as well as the warmth and charm of her personality.

A new production of *Lakmé* was mounted for Joan and the opera proved to be a great vehicle for the Company, with the title role subsequently sung by Joan Carden and Rhonda Bruce. A disastrous fire in the storehouse destroyed the entire produc-tion only a year or so after the premiére, which was a great pity as the piece provided so many good roles for our singers.

The Company at this time consisted of forty soloists and a chorus of forty-seven.

The Elizabethan Trust Orchestra which had its own management always played for
the opera, although we had often to engage extra players to reinforce their meagre
numbers, a situation which caused untold trouble over the years. Of course, the
orchestra should have been part of the opera organisation but, for insane and unfath-
omable reasons, it took until 1989 for this to even begin to eventuate.

Lakmé was new to Australia; audiences here had not before experienced this ori-
ental spectacular. The public and many of the critics loved it but a few of the hide-
bound couldn't abide it!

Nadine Amadio in *The Financial Review*:

> 'Fine and delicate musical theatre. Richard Bonynge conducted superbly with such con-
> trolled vitality and such insight ... (his) involvement with French opera is a generously
> shared enthusiasm that offers great, musical delights to Australian audiences.'

In *The Australian*, Maria Prerauer thought

Right: Huguette Tourangeau as Carmen
with Donald Smith as Don José

'Great singing was back at the *Lakmé* première … those beautiful full-throated sounds that used to distinguish grand opera from the spoken word but which seems to have gone out of fashion recently.'

Linda Phillips thought she had

'never heard the famous Bell Song sung with such warmth, beauty and brilliance.'

Roger Covell wrote in *The Sydney Morning Herald:*

'Miss Sutherland's voice manifests itself in a state of flawless and remarkable steadiness of tone.'

David Ahern in *The Daily Telegraph:*

'The creamy richness of her voice was best displayed in the soft, translucent succulence of Delibes' melodies.'

Elizabeth Silsbury in *The Adelaide Morning Daily* thought Joan's

'first few notes that floated in from off-stage were unearthly magic.'

and that Richard Bonynge's

'musical direction was expert, affording loving care way beyond what the score deserved

… *Lakmé* is the preposterous opera par excellence.'

In the incestuous way of the Australian music world Elizabeth later became a member of our Board. This charming lady carried a torch for Alban Berg's *Lulu*. 'I'll put it on if you'll pay for the empty seats' I told her. I don't think I was ever popular with the Australian 'cognoscenti' — I saw no need to educate the public, only to fill the house and entertain.

I lured Clifford Grant, the Australian bass, back to sing Lakmé's father Nilakantha, and Roger Covell agreed that this 'bass of splendid promise in the 1965 Sutherland Bonynge tour … has now imposingly fulfilled that promise'.

Felix Werder got in one of his 'digs' at the opera:

> 'In this popera, The Australian Popera certainly shows its indulgence for vulgar taste and unlimited spending.'

Fortunate we were to have the money to spend, after the losses on his opera, *The Affair*, which sold a dismal 26.4 per cent of the available tickets.

The National Times thought I

> 'drew such luscious sounds from the orchestra that it was a crying shame they weren't playing something more worth the effort'.

As Orlovsky says, '*Chacun à son gout*'!

Norman Ayrton directed and Desmond Digby produced exotic sets, costuming the piece in the 1860s to heighten the contrast between the British Raj and the native Hindus. This didn't please everyone either, and Roger Covell thought that 'the temple and its flower garden looked as if someone had tipped a fruit and vegetable barrow over an old band rotunda'.

The Australian Opera's finest were on show — the Raj Quintet sung by Isobel Buchanan, Jennifer Bermingham, Rosina Raisbeck, John Pringle and Henri Wilden, Clifford Grant as Nilakantha and Mallika and Hadji by Huguette Tourangeau and Graeme Ewer. The cast remained the same throughout this run, except for the Quintet which was played for four performances by Anson Austin as the hero Gérald, his brother officer Frédéric by Pieter van der Stolk, the two English girls (Ellen and Rose) by Beryl Furlan and Cynthia Johnston and the governess by Mary Hayman.

The opera almost didn't get on at all. The Trust Orchestra, protesting at the threatened reduction of their numbers owing to budget cuts, staged a strike and stayed out approximately half-an-hour before beginning the opera. We were more than sympathetic toward the hard-working and conscientious bunch of players, but what a hell of a time for their management to choose!

According to *The Sun Herald*, 'the Governor-General attended and was screamed at rudely', but I can't for the life of me remember why, unless it was because he'd had the task of pitch-forking Gough Whitlam out of office.

We played ten *Lakmés*, one of which was televised, between 10 July and 13 August, during which time I opened with the next new production, *Carmen*, on 31 July, conducting the first six performances. The luscious Mlle Tourangeau was Carmen and there were three scheduled Don Josés. Donald Smith was unfortunately the victim of illness just before opening night but Ronald Stevens took over with great personal success. Later on Nicola Filacuridi (who had sung with Joan at Glyndebourne in *I Puritani* in 1960), now living in Sydney, came out of retirement for a couple of performances. Isobel Buchanan, well on her way to becoming a darling of the public, had a big success as Micaela and was doubled in the role by Dolores Cambridge, who a little later would leave The Australian Opera to join one of the German companies — Cassel, I believe.

Raymond Myers and Pieter van der Stolk both sang Escamillo. Myers was an old favourite with the public; van der Stolk was new to the Company that year. A Dutchman married to the Australian soprano, Joy Mammen, he had worked with us in the television shows *Who's Afraid of Opera?* A thinking artist and a superb actor, his voice had an insistent vibrato which became rather more noticeable when he was uneasy. Certain critics and members of the public disliked this and he frequently received a great deal of flak. I found his performances extraordinarily intelligent and moving and the fact that he was with the Company until a recurrent back problem necessitated his retirement proves that I was not alone. Carmen's gypsy friend, Frasquita, was shared by Cynthia Johnston and Beryl Furlan, and Mercedes sung by Etela Piha. Dancairo was performed by both Ronald Maconaghie and Robert Eddie, and Remendado by Graeme Ewer and Gordon Wilcock. Gregory Yurisich, just beginning his career (he sang Henry VIII in concert performances of *Anna Bolena* with us in New York, Washington and Boston in 1985) sang Morales.

The opera was produced and designed by Tom Lingwood, then resident designer, and his economical sets made the small stage of the Sydney Opera House seem enormous. The public always enjoys *Carmen* and the press, as we were soon to find out, was divided as usual. Nadine Amadio wrote in *The Financial Review*:

'This was a glowingly beautiful performance with the honours going almost entirely to
the conductor, Richard Bonynge ... there was never a moment when the fascinating
unfolding of the score did not hold the attention and move the emotion with its fine
attention to detail. A delicate but very insistent tension held the work together magnificently ... How extraordinary that an Australian conductor should so perfectly capture
that silken evocation of the French dream of exotic romance. It is a subtle and elusive
quality and Bonynge can communicate it better than any conductor performing to-day
... the orchestra played superbly under Bonynge and gave a memorable performance.'

David Ahern in *The Sunday Telegraph* thought

'Mr Bonynge's absurdly fast tempos right from the overture made most of the opera seem
farcical, exaggerated and lollipop'.

Maria Prerauer in *The Australian* considered:

'I do not think Bonynge's speeds are too fast. Occasionally they are too slow!'

Above: Lakmé Quintet Act 1. Cynthia Johnston as Rose, Anson Austin as Gérald, Beryl Furlan as Ellen, Mary Hayman as the Governess and Pieter van der Stolk as Frédéric

The same lady thought Tourangeau's

'middle to low registers are the most gorgeously rich, round, dark and sensuous in captivity'.

Alan Farrelly in *The Sun* found Miss Tourangeau

'a most bewitching Carmen with the sultriest voice I've heard'.

My last opera in the winter season was *The Marriage of Figaro*. Having prepared the revival I was able to stay for only two performances, owing to overseas commitments. During my term with The Australian Opera I generally spent about five months (split into two periods) with the Company — roughly half the working year. I think my absence was a good thing as I would always see and hear with fresh eyes and ears on my return.

I loved conducting *Figaro* in this elegant John Copley production and with a splendid cast.

'Last night *Figaro* was dazzling'

wrote Alan Farrelly in *The Sun*.

'What wit, what spectacle, what fun … the overall stylistic framework was so unshakeably correct,'

said Maria Prerauer.

And Roger Covell:

'I came away from the performance feeling the kind of renewal and refreshment which a good performance of *Figaro* always encourages.'

Isobel Buchanan sang The Countess, Cynthia Johnston — Susanna, Jennifer Bermingham — Cherubino, Rosina Raisbeck — Marcellina, Ronald Maconaghie — Figaro, John Pringle — The Count, Graeme Ewer — Basilio, Neil-Warren Smith — Bartolo, Gordon Wilcock — Don Curzio, Donald Solomon — Antonio and Luise Napier — Barbarina. Janice Hill and Catherine Elliott were the Bridesmaids.

On 8 August, in company with Huguette Tourangeau, John Pringle and Henri Wilden, we gave a concert at Government House in the presence of His Excellency the Governor of New South Wales and Lady Cutler, the proceeds of which went to the Royal New South Wales Institute for Deaf and Blind Children.

I returned to the Company in October to be with them for their first overseas tour, conducting four *Rigolettos* in Wellington, New Zealand. The orchestra pit of the acoustically splendid Victorian theatre was so small that I had perforce to perch on a bench in the front row of the stalls and some of the orchestra overflowed into the boxes. The electrical system failed twice during the opening night. Just after Gilda's entrance — total blackness; Joan Carden, singing Gilda, had to remount the stairs and make her entrance again when the lights came on. At the end of the opera the electrically operated curtain failed and the unfortunate Gilda had to climb out of the sack in full view of the public to take her calls!

Isobel Buchanan sang her first Gildas on this tour, sharing the part with Joan Carden. Reginald Byers and Henri Wilden sang the Duke, Raymond Myers and Robert Allman, Rigoletto. Maddelena was Margreta Elkins, whom I had encouraged back from England to join the Company, Sparafucile was Neil Warren-Smith, and Monterone was sung by Grant Dickson.

Our activities in the Southern Hemisphere this year included two recitals in Adelaide, one in Sydney and one in Canberra during August, and we made a concert tour (May-June) with the New Zealand Symphony Orchestra to Wellington, Auckland, Christchurch, Dunedin, Napier and Palmerston North, thoroughly enjoying that beautiful country between the ten concerts.

The year finished with an unforgettable event, 'The Rights of a Child' concert presented by the Australian Government on 12 December in the General Assembly Hall of the United Nations in New York. The total receipts of the concert went to UNICEF for the benefit of the world's needy children. The artistic director was Robert Helpmann, the hosts Zoe Caldwell and Cyril Ritchard, and among those taking part with us were Rolf Harris, June Bronhill, John Meehan, Marilyn Rowe and Marjorie Lawrence. Joan sang the final scene from *La Sonnambula* and 'Ah fors' è lui' from *La Traviata* but our memory is of Marjorie Lawrence courageously singing 'Waltzing Matilda' from her wheel-chair.

4

NINETEEN SEVENTY SEVEN

T his year was the first for which I felt an overall responsibility and the Company gave 231 performances of 21 operas. As Brian Hoad wrote in *The Bulletin*:

Facing Page: Lucrezia Borgia Act 2 with Robert Allman as Don Alfonso

'Bonynge has made a promising start ... planning his first major season in Australia to present a nicely balanced cross-section of the art in its golden age from Mozart's *Cosi fan tutte* (1790) to Puccini's *Suor Angelica* (1918), balancing the light tunefulness of Auber's *Fra Diavolo* against the heavy drama of Verdi's *Macbeth*, or the glitter of Rossini's *Barber* against the Teutonic gloom of Wagner's *Dutchman*.'

In addition to the above operas of which *Fra Diavolo*, *Macbeth* (with Elizabeth Connell), the *Dutchman* (with Lone Koppel-Winther), and *Madama Butterfly* (with Leona Mitchell) were new, there was also a new production of Donizetti's *Lucrezia Borgia*, as well as revivals of *Lakmé*, *Carmen*, *Bohème*, *Tosca*, *Aida*, *Magic Flute*, *Figaro*, *Fidelio*, *Albert Herring*, *Hoffman*, *Pagliacci*, *Suor Angelica*, *The Mikado* and *Gondoliers*. *Parsifal* was given in concert form and a special performance of *Albert Herring* was given in memory of Benjamin Britten on 13 March in the presence of Her Majesty The Queen and His Royal Highness The Duke of Edinburgh.

I was in Sydney for the beginning of the year and spent several weeks preparing the revivals of *Carmen* and *Lakmé*, although I was only able to stay for two performances of each. Changes of cast from the previous season included Heather Begg as Carmen, Lone Koppel-Winther as Micaela, Elizabeth Fretwell as Frasquita and Lyndon Terracini as Morales. In *Lakmé*, Joan Carden appeared as the heroine and Robert Allman as Nilakantha with Margreta Elkins as Mallika. That The Australian Opera is able to double and treble cast is one of its great strengths and the only way a company so far from the rest of the world can exist. It means the singers and *répétiteurs* have to work hard and it also means the show always goes on. London may get a last-minute replacement from Hamburg or Vienna, New York from Boston or San Francisco, but New Zealand and Fiji are hardly brimming over with operatic replacements, and neither are the other capital cities of Australia.

Disaster struck just before Easter in the form of a warehouse fire and a great deal of the sets and costumes of *La Forza del Destino*, *Madama Butterfly*, *Figaro*, *Bohème*, *Merry Widow* and *Mikado* were destroyed, taxing the Company's tottering finances to the hilt. Most of these would be soon remade as they were an essential part of the repertoire, but *Forza* would have to wait until 1988.

Above: Costume design by Kristian
Fredrikson for Gennaro, Act 2
Right: As Lucrezia Borgia, Act 3

Above: As Suor Angelica
Left: Suor Angelica (left to right)
Catherine Elliott, Lois Empey, Mary
Hayman, Cynthia Johnston, Joan
Sutherland

I returned in the winter season for *Lucrezia Borgia,* the first Australian performance of this opera in the twentieth century. George Ogilvie directed and Kristian
Fredrikson designed a stunning production; because of the numerous roles it contained it proved a great vehicle for the Company (as well as the star). Of course there
was the usual advance speculation as to what muck I'd dredged up from 'the rag bags
of the nineteenth century' but the success of the performances killed this and many
of the critics decided it was a good opera after all.

Lindsay Brown in *The Sun-Herald:*

> 'The Australian Opera's opening night of *Lucrezia Borgia* safely banished various suspi-
> cions that Donizetti is too much of a light-weight to launch any season of large-scale pre-
> tension. Indeed, all departments of the performance seemed in conspiracy to affirm
> Donizetti's magnitude and weightiness.'

W.L. Hoffman in *The Canberra Times:*

> 'Some of the Sydney music critics, more noted for their clichés than for musical perspi-
> cacity have exhibited a somewhat sneering disparagement of Donizetti's operas as a
> whole ... but Donizetti ... was one of the great figures in the history of opera, as this
> *Lucrezia Borgia* shows, both musically and dramatically. It just takes very great singing to
> bring his operas to life ... in all ways this is a notable and memorable production.'

David Malouf in *The National Times:*

> 'It's customary for opera seasons to open with productions of great splendour in which the
> capacities of the Company are on extended view. The Australian Opera's *Lucrezia Borgia*
> is all that and more. Musically it is perhaps the best thing it has ever done ... Sutherland's
> performance was one of the most powerful I have encountered in the opera theatre. She
> was responsive at every point to the musical possibilities of what she had to sing; and that

Above: Joan Sutherland as Suor Angelica and Rosina Raisbeck as the Princess

is to say to the dramatic possibilities as well, since in Donizetti they are one. Her range is breathtaking; both the range of her voice … her low 'morto' in the last aria is as astonishing as anything at the top of her register … and the range of what she expressed, from melting pathos to the most chilling menace. The instant she steps on the stage the public responds not only to the voice but to the mystical aura as well.'

Maria Prerauer in *The Australian:*

'Go, sit back and have something to tell your grandchildren in the year 2,000.'

Gregg Curran in *Nation Review:*

'Joan Sutherland is, as ever, a phenomenon. Maturity has been kind to her and she looks fine and far more interesting than she used to. She is vocally, in her prime … truly a force of nature.'

Roger Covell in *The Sydney Morning Herald:*

'Happy were those fecund days in the 1830s when Donizetti could dash off *Lucrezia Borgia* in a month and still make a solid job of it. Happy too (though there are, alas, no more Donizettis) the opera company which can revive *Lucrezia* with Sutherland to sing the title role and Bonynge to conduct. Skill and sympathy are at ease with each other in such a situation.'

Nadine Amadio in *The Financial Review* wrote of Joan's

'performance of profound professionalism and opulent beauty' … (she) 'showed what *bel canto* is all about … the most ravishing singing in the world. From the pit Richard Bonynge drew superb playing from the Elizabethan Symphony Orchestra. The orchestra always seems more musical, more sparkling and more theatrically aware under Bonynge.'

Frank Harris in *The Mirror:*

'Let's have no more argument about unfamiliar operas being introduced. *Lucrezia* has all the ingredients of a public winner.'

There were ten sold-out performances with young and not so young people sleeping outside the Opera House to be sure of standing passes. The cast was very fine. Robert Allman played Lucrezia's husband Don Alfonso, Ronald Stevens and Paul Ferris alternated as her son Gennaro, and the young nobleman, Orsini, was Margreta Elkins. The four Venetian nobles were played by Robin Donald, Lyndon Terracini, Gregory Yurisich and Lamberto Furlan, with Graeme Ewer as Rustighello, John Germain as Astolfo, Pieter van der Stolk as Gubetta and lovely Josephine Bermingham as the Princess Negroni.

During the run of *Borgia* we played six performances of Rossini's *Barber* and I enjoyed the constant change from melodrama to comedy. We had a fine cast — Huguette Tourangeau sang Rosina, John Pringle — Figaro, Paul Ferris — Almaviva, Clifford Grant — Basilio, Alan Light — Bartolo, Mary Hayman and Donald Solomon — Berta and Ambrogio, Lyndon Terracini and Joseph Grunfelder — Fiorello and the Officer. Michael Beauchamp restaged John Cox's original production with designs by Roger Butlin.

The reviews were mixed as they generally were, no matter who or what, but we

enjoyed it and so did the public.

'What fun! What splendid entertainment … That's style for you,'

wrote *The Australian's* Maria Prerauer.

Roger Covell (*The Sydney Morning Herald*) liked Huguette's

'low notes projected in a kind of chalumeau register as if she had just pulled them, freshly browned, out of the lower drawer in an oven … for real wit it was necessary to refer to the musical direction of Richard Bonynge, which reminded us time and time again what the stage action failed to do; that this was a comedy whose smiles come from a combination of lithe precision and sudden effervescence … I cling to the memory of Bonynge's adroit conducting, to bursts of vivid impersonation by Pringle and to the astonishing contrast in the mobile voice of Tourangeau.'

For the record, she sang 'Cruda sorte' from Rossini's *Italiana* in the lesson scene.

The Sun opined that

'For some unknown reason The Australian Opera is using the full Italian text.'

Above: The Barber of Seville Act 1
Finale. (Left to right foreground) Berta
— Mary Hayman; Rosina — Huguette
Tourangeau; Paul Ferris — Almaviva;
John Pringle — Figaro; Alan Light —
Bartolo; and Clifford Grant — Basilio

'Nothing is sacred in this delightful, artificial romp,'

wrote Maria Prerauer of Auber's *Fra Diavolo*, our next new production, and of its star Isobel Buchanan,

> 'she tosses off with elan her coloratura showpieces ... to score the personal triumph of the première.'

Brian Hoad in *The Bulletin:*

> 'A fine bit of French frivolity. The choice ... is a great success. And for a change patrons may be seen currently leaving the Opera House with a song or two in their hearts as well as a twinkle in the eye ... For *Fra Diavolo* no expense had been spared and the investment has paid off handsomely.'

Australian critics were often preoccupied with costs, sometimes with opposing views:

H.R. Forst in *The Sunday Telegraph:*

> 'After footing the bill for this colossal extravaganza our Opera should not be heard again crying for help and money. No financial optimism could hope to cover the expenses for

the lavish costumes and sets in the number of listed performance dates as well as the fees for conductor Richard Bonynge and producer John Copley.'

Above: Fra Diavolo Costume design by Michael Stennett for the soldiers

John earned his money five times over with the very witty production which was complemented by Henry Bardon's sets and Michael Stennett's costumes.

Brian Hoad in *The Bulletin*:

'John Copley has the right mixture of wit and good humour, a deep affection for all opera (grand or comique) and a polished sense of style, all of which the opera needs and gets. The severe stage of the Opera House has been transformed into a colourful cardboard cut-out version of an early nineteenth-century theatre … When the curtain rises we are in Italy of the romantic dreamtime … pretty mountains, charming villages and "natural-istic" sylvan glades painted on flats which can be whirled away to capture that sense of theatrical enchantment and magical transformation which was the epitome of popular theatre of the day.'

Nadine Amadio in *The Financial Review*:

Above: Fra Diavolo Act 1. (Foreground Left to right) Dennis Olsen and Heather Begg as Lord and Lady Allcash, Isobel Buchanan as Zerlina, Anson Austin as Lorenzo and Robert Gard as Fra Diavolo

'Australian Opera's champagne for the season. Over recent years the wide version of Bonynge's musical activities, both here and abroad, his versatility and extreme professionalism, and his concern and understanding of the singers and musicians who work with him have given him an enviable international reputation. His remarkable ability to project the very life force of the music he conducts to his audience has earned him the title of Australia's Mr Music … Bonynge's glittering performance, stylishly French and full of the atmosphere of the period, was the most outstanding contribution to the work. It pointed the wit, whipped up the froth and constantly bubbled and sparkled under the vocal lines … The involvement of a fine cast of principals led to some superb ensemble singing displaying the craft behind Auber's froth …'

The cast was indeed fine. Both the tenors, Robert Gard as Diavolo and Anson Austin as Lorenzo were able to cope with fiendishly high *tessitura*. Heather Begg and Dennis Olsen were a precious comic duo as Milord and Milady, while Graeme Ewer and Neil Warren Smith played Beppo and Giacomo as an Italo-Australiano version of Laurel and Hardy. Donald Shanks was the Innkeeper and Conal Coad a Peasant. I had the pleasure of conducting the first five performances and there were sixteen given that season. It has remained in the repertoire and was revived for the third time in 1988.

On 24 July practically the entire company of singers gave an operatic gala in aid of the Royal NSW Institute for Deaf and Blind Children in the Concert Hall of the Sydney Opera House, with Sharolyn Kimmorley and myself doing our best to provide accompaniments on two pianos. They sang a very lengthy programme of ensembles, mostly from operas not in the repertoire including *Ernani, La Sonnambula, Saffo, Esclarmonde, Martha, L'Oracolo, La Rondine, L'Amico Fritz, I Lombardi, L'Italiana in Algeri, Il Matrimonio Segreto, Poliuto, La Périchole, Der Tsarevich, Ruddigore* and *The Bohemian Girl*. Item number 23 was programmed a surprise trio and Rosina Raisbeck, Heather Begg and Joan (she being the shortest of these three Amazonian ladies) sang for the first and last time together 'Three Little Maids from School' from *The Mikado*. The public probably had a good attack of operatic indigestion but we had good fun and a good cause was served.

The one sad occurrence of the season was the resignation of John Winther, who left to become head of the Conservatorium in Newcastle. He and the board had had serious disagreements. I missed John. He was a gentleman in his dealings with the artists and he had great theatrical flair and could always see both sides of the coin, something I tried to learn from him.

The Board of Directors, led by their Chairman, Charles Berg, precipitately chose a new manager, Peter Hemmings, who had lately left the Scottish Opera. He had applied for the job of General Manager with the Toronto Opera but their Board chose Lotfi Mansouri which left him free to set his sights on Australia.

Having landed the job, his first plans for Australia, he decided, were to change Joan's repertoire. She would sing Gloriana in Britten's opera of the same name, also Lady Billows in *Albert Herring* and Emilia in *The Makropoulos Case*. The paper would disintegrate if I were to reproduce Madame's comments. Throughout his few years

Right: Heather Begg as Carmen

with The Australian Opera he would constantly try to do my job rather than his own.

The season ended for us on a very happy note, although 'happy' is hardly the word for Puccini's *Suor Angelica*. It was performed as the second half of a double bill with Leoncavallo's *Pagliacci* — the latter was not generally deemed a success, despite some good performances. Sergei Baigildin was Canio, Robert Allman — Tonio, Beryl Furlan — Nedda, John Pringle — Silvio, and Graeme Ewer — Beppe.

Suor Angelica was a great vehicle for the ladies in the Company: they loved it and their devotion to the opera shone through in each of the four performances we gave.

Rosina Raisbeck's titanic presence as the Princess made a great foil for Joan and our leading singers lavished great care in the many small roles: Isobel Buchanan as the Nursing Sister, Elizabeth Fretwell as the Monitress, Heather Begg as the Abbess, Cynthia Johnston as Suor Genovieffa, Lesley Stender as the Mistress of the Novices, Kathleen Moore as Suor Osmina, Mary Jane Corderoy as Suor Dolcina, Miluska Simkova the Portress, Narelle Davidson and Rosemary Gunn the Lay Sisters, Judith

Saliba, Luise Napier and Hellen O'Rourke as the Novices, Lois Empey and Mary Hayman as the Alms Sisters, Catherine Elliott as another nun, Josephine Bermingham as the Madonna and Gregory Howett as the Child. I must mention them all because the extraordinarily moving performances were the result of their dedication and their working together as a company. This revival was designed by Desmond Digby and directed by Moffatt Oxenbould, who had done the whole *Trittico* some years earlier. He directed only rarely, which was a pity as he worked so sympathetically with the cast.

The Press seemed genuinely surprised at the impact Joan made as Angelica which was natural as she had not sung any of the *verismo* repertoire before in Australia. However, as H.R. Forst remembered in *The Sunday Telegraph:*

Above: Fra Diavolo Act 3 Robert Gard as Fra Diavolo

'The once-in-a-lifetime coloratura superstructure that made Joan Sutherland stupendous has always been based on a sound dramatic vocal foundation ... Her emotional outburst at the climax of the one-act opera displayed irresistible power and a rare volume of exquisite resonance.'

Maria Prerauer wrote

'She lets fly notes that are in themselves charged with *verismo* emotion ... (she) offers up her voice with all the stops out. The result is sensational.'

Frank Harris in *The Mirror* thought

'She turned Puccini's generally despised and rejected *Angelica* into what he always rated it — a triumph among his several masterpieces ... the whole work was restored almost miraculously to the magic Puccini imagined when he wrote it.'

Brian Hoad felt that Joan as Angelica was

'a singer in a role which is totally matched to voice and temperament ... it resulted in the sort of total theatrical experience which only opera at its finest can throw up from time to time ... The interplay with her sister nuns is ensemble work at its most sensitive. The explosive meeting with her aunt is played out with all the new-found dramatic power of her lower registers. And in the closing scene the more familiar Sutherland soars heavenwards as only she can.'

Roger Covell considered *Angelica*

'... lustrous and moving in its revival ... (Joan Sutherland) threw herself into the physical representation of hope, anguish and despair wholeheartedly, holding nothing back in dramatic effort ... The other shining ingredient of the performance was Richard Bonynge's conducting, sensitive and reticent where necessary but always pursuing the line of Puccini's lyrical singers with sinewy emphasis. The same kind of conducting virtues made the orchestral contribution to *Pagliacci* its most eloquent asset.'

I returned once more during the year, this time to visit Brisbane for the first time since 1965, conducting *Carmen* with my old friend Margreta Elkins in the title role, Isobel Buchanan as Micaëla, Ronald Stevens as José and Pieter van der Stolk as Escamillo. *Theatre Australia* reported that '*During its November visit to Brisbane the Australian Opera drew its best crowds in that city for nearly a decade*'.

5

NINETEEN SEVENTY EIGHT

The year began with a lavish new *Merry Widow* designed for the Concert Hall of the Opera House by Kristian Fredrikson and directed by Lotfi Mansouri. The stage of the Concert Hall was transformed into an art-nouveau palace with a colossal staircase which camouflaged the great organ. Some critics were antiquatedly toffee-nosed about operetta in the repertoire of an opera company, but the thirteen fully subscribed houses (the Concert Hall holds nearly 3,000) made for a healthy start to the year. In fact, there were huge lines of standees at each of the performances during January and February.

The cast included Ronald Stevens as Danilo, Anson Austin — Camille, Gordon Wilcock — Baron Zeta, Graeme Ewer — Njegus, Isobel Buchanan — Valencienne, Paul Ferris and Robert Eddie as St Brioche and Cascada, Etela Piha, Cynthia Johnston and Rosina Raisbeck as Olga, Sylviane and Praskovia, Alan Light, John Germain and Donald Solomon as the three ambassadorial stooges. Heather Begg played Zozo, the can-can dancer in the last act.

We based our performances on the 1907 version which Lehár made for Daly's theatre in London, with the added song for Njegus in Act III and the added character of Zozo, who sings Valencienne's original number in the third act. Douglas Gamley arranged a splendid overture, and a ballet for Act III.

David Gyger wrote in *Opera Australia*:

> 'Joan Sutherland makes a magnificent Widow ... she sang, acted, danced and talked ... her way through Lehár's classic operetta role ... with absolute aplomb. Her's was a virtuoso performance that really did bring to life the character of Anna Glawari ... It was something of a paradox that Sutherland herself, who has often been criticised for her incomprehensibility got the words across best of anyone — whether she was singing or speaking.'

Brian Hoad wrote in *The Bulletin*:

> 'Having died no less than six different types of unpleasant deaths many times over in Sydney in recent years ... Joan Sutherland needs and gets a break in a spectacular new production of Lehár's deathless operetta ... Her sense of fun is irresistibly contagious, her warmth is palpable, her romantic affections naively touching and sincere and she sings like the legendary Pontevedrian nightingale.'

Above: *The Merry Widow* Act 3 Zozo
(Heather Begg)
Facing Page: The Merry Widow Act 1

Above: The Merry Widow Act 2 (Left to right) Paul Ferris, Robert Eddie, Gordon Wilcock, Donald Solomon, Ron Stevens, Graeme Ewer, John Germain, Alan Light

Nadine Amadio in *The Financial Review*:

'If anything ever confirmed the brilliant stage-craft and the wide repertoire of the remarkable Joan Sutherland it was this portrayal of the *Widow* ... Her amused and tolerant sophistication was underlined by her occasional head-thrown-back laugh which had all the beauty and flair of a modern Garbo. It seems that once again one of the most musically productive partnerships in the world of opera, that of Sutherland and Bonynge, has notched another victory.'

H.R. Forst, in *The Daily Telegraph*:

'Almost certainly Vilia has never been sung quite as beautifully before and other numbers, too, sound unique in radiance and splendour ... Lehar would have felt greatly honoured to include our phenomenal Joan Sutherland in the list of his interpreters.'

Maria Prerauer deplored Joan wasting herself in the *Widow* and, along with some others, carped about the cost. This annoyed Robert Morley who at the time was appearing in Australia and he wrote to *The Australian*:

'It is the function of your theatre critic surely to appraise the performance he attends, not to pine wistfully for another fare. In disparaging the choice of *The Merry Widow* as a suit-

able vehicle for your great opera star he ignores the thousands who, like myself, loathe and detest grand opera and were stunned into delight by the knowledge that we were going to watch and hear the wonderful tunes sung by Miss Sutherland.

In all the years I have been coming here I have never seen anything in this always unpredictable country that so warmed my heart or filled me with admiration as this production.

Of course it must have cost a fortune, of course the money could have been spent on other projects — it always can — but to those who, like myself, were lucky enough to be there it was a one-in-a-lifetime experience, and they are almost always expensive.'

As I write (1988) we are in the midst of the fourth revival of *The Widow* with many of the original cast — Ronald Stevens, Anson Austin, Gordon Wilcock, Graeme Ewer and Rosina Raisbeck aged seventy-two playing her inimitable Praskovia. I first saw this grand lady as the mother in *The Tales of Hoffmann* in 1944. I asked Rosina if she minded my mentioning her age, but she said, 'On the contrary, I'm proud of it!' And well she might be.

After *The Widow*, came four performances of *Nabucco*. This was a new production by Bernd Benthaak with new sets by Tom Lingwood but costumes from the old production. Lone Koppel-Winther sang Abigaille, Robert Allman — Nabucco, Donald Shanks — Zaccaria, Margreta Elkins — Fenena, Lamberto Furlan — Ismaele, Mary Hayman — Anna, Kevin Mills — Abdallo and Joseph Grunfelder the High Priest.

Above Top: The Merry Widow Act 1
Above: In Act 2 *The Merry Widow*

In November of this same year I conducted four performances of the same opera in Adelaide at the Festival Theatre and two in Melbourne in the huge St Kilda Palais. Rita Hunter made her Australian début in Adelaide as Abigaille and scored a big success both there and in Melbourne. The cast was otherwise the same as Sydney, except for Mary-Jane Corderoy in the role of Anna.

John Sinclair writing in *The Melbourne Herald* thought the production

'would have commanded respect anywhere in world! ... (Rita Hunter) sang with memorable accuracy and brilliance ... the chorus were better than in 1973 and, under Richard Bonynge's intense and precise direction, the Elizabethan Sydney Orchestra produced the best orchestral sound I have heard in an Australian Opera production for years.'

At the beginning of the Sydney winter season I conducted eight performances of *The Marriage of Figaro* in the Copley production rehearsed by Michael Beauchamp.

Right: During the dress rehearsal of
The Merry Widow. Richard Bonynge
with (left to right) Isobel Buchanan,
Etela Piha and Cynthia Johnston

The cast was somewhat the same as the 1976 revival, except for Glenys Fowles as Susanna, Eilene Hannan as Cherubino, Melinda Sharman as Barbarina and Robert Gard as Basilio. Nance Grant took over the last three Countesses from Isobel Buchanan and Grant Dickson sang the last three Bartolos.

Frank Harris wrote:

'From Bonynge's first bars in the overture, one sensed immediately a top performance.'

Isobel's performance was thought much matured and there was praise for Glenys

Above: The Merry Widow Act 2 Rosina
Raisbeck as Praskovia and Ron Stevens
as Danilo
Left: The Merry Widow Act 2

Fowles, John Pringle and Ronald Maconaghie. Rosina Raisbeck and Neil Warren-
Smith were as splendid a Marcellina and Bartolo as one could desire. There were
thirteen performances between 5 July and 26 August.

Following *Figaro* came a new production of *Norma*, an opera not heard in
Australia for more than sixty years.

Sandro Sequi, who had directed it for us at Covent Garden and later with
Montserrat Caballé at the Orange Festival, made his Australian début and the sets
and costumes were by Fiorella Mariani. Between 5 July and 26 August we gave thir-
teen performances. Adalgisa was shared by Margreta Elkins and Heather Begg,
Ronald Stevens was Pollione, Clifford Grant and Donald Shanks shared Oroveso,
Paul Ferris and Trevor Brown — Flavio, and Etela Piha sang Clotilde.

'An evening of a lifetime of opera-going'

was Brian Hoad's headline in *The Bulletin:*

> 'The audience is drawn into the private emotional turmoil of a woman crossed in love.
> Love and hate, compassion and fury, past happiness and present sorrow, base thoughts
> and noble action fluctuate violently through her. And Sutherland masters the dramatic
> and vocal complexities to perfection … The vast humanity she radiates seems to fire the
> whole production. It is the sort of magical performance rarely found even in a lifetime of
> opera-going. It is the sort of performance which left its audience for the most part dumb-

Above Top: Nabucco Rita Hunter as Abigaille and Robert Allman as Nabucco
Above: Nabucco Lona Koppel as Abigaille and Joseph Grunfelder as the High Priest

founded, precipitating one of the wildest receptions the Sydney Opera House has ever witnessed or is likely to for a long time.'

'Sutherland at her very best' was H.R. Forst's headline in *The Daily Telegraph:*

'Just the part to show her voice of the century in its most startling aspects … If you want to hear La Stupenda and what really has made her stupendous, this is the opera to choose.'

In *The Sydney Morning Herald*, Roger Covell wrote of

'the unfailing flow of lustrous and substantial tone she delivers throughout an evening of the most challenging vocal demands … Sutherland impersonates her always as a woman strong in passion but never a monster or a tigress. The womanliness is in her manner and, above all, in a voice as beautiful as it is sure and agile. Don't miss *Norma* if you care about opera. It is a rare opportunity to see and hear the greatest living interpreter of the part in an inimitable performance.'

Lindsay Brown wrote of

'the superbly incomparable resource of Miss Sutherland … Her exquisitely light and parenthetic coloratura in the Casta Diva aria, done with the scrupulous artistry that excludes excesses of mere grandstanding, and the remarkable depth and darkness of some near contralto phrases in Act 2, were signals that the peaks are still very much within Miss Sutherland's reach … The generosity of her attitude in duet scenes with soprano Margreta Elkins was unmistakable.'

Nadine Amadio in *The Financial Review* thought *Norma*

> 'the musical event of a lifetime'

Above: Norma Act 1 with Clifford Grant as Oroveso and Ronald Stevens as Pollione

and spoke of

> 'Sutherland's amazing vocal gifts and her deeply involved and humane acting ... Richard Bonynge was the source of all security and support for the singers. He drew a world-class performance from the orchestra. One almost felt the spirit of Bellini residing in this remarkable Australian conductor, who has revived and renewed the very essence of *bel-canto* opera in the world to-day. There was an amazing fusion between Sutherland and Bonynge, particularly in the last act, when together they lifted the music to the summit of heroic power and grandeur.'

We were very happy to know that *Norma* was so much appreciated. *Norma* is undoubtedly Joan's favourite of all her roles and Bellini is very close to our hearts.

During the run of *Norma* I prepared a new production of *Don Giovanni* and performed it eight times between 19 July and 8 August. The Don was James Morris in his Australian début, Donna Anna was Joan Carden, Elvira — Lone Koppel-Winther, Zerlina — Isobel Buchanan, Ottavio — Henri Wilden, Leporello — Neil Warren-Smith, Commendatore — Donald Shanks and Masetto — Lyndon Terracini. Hugh Coleman designed the sets, Kristian Fredrikson the costumes and George Ogilvie was the director.

> 'At last, the *Don Giovanni* we have all been waiting for,'

wrote Maria Prerauer in *The Australian*.

'Wednesday's Sydney Opera House première was the Australian Opera's third attempt … and this time they made it.'

She was besotted over James Morris...

'… looking uncannily like a handsome young Errol Flynn … surely destined soon to become the world's foremost Don Juan.'

Brian Hoad wrote in *The Bulletin*:

'As a change from all the super canaries flying in this season, The Australian Opera has imported for this occasion an impressive piece of beefcake with a mighty voice, James Morris, a young American bass-baritone fresh from some triumphant *Giovanni*'s in New York. His is a performance of great style and confidence, both vocally and dramatically.'

He also complimented

'a particularly strong ensemble under the guidance of Richard Bonynge in the pit … here is a realisation of *Mozart* as succeessful as the current *Figaro* revival. *Giovanni*, of course, is a much harder and heavier nut to crack — and although it has taken The Australian Opera a decade to do so, the contents were well worth waiting for.'

Above: La Traviata Act 3. Kiri te Kanawa as Violetta
Left: Don Giovanni Act 1. Isobel Buchanan (Zerlina) and Lyndon Terracini (Masetto) and James Morris (the Don)

Roger Covell wrote in *The Sydney Morning Herald:*

'If we had to wait until now for The Australian Opera to produce a cogent and vivid *Don Giovanni*, the wait has proved amply worthwhile. Casting from strength, the Company has brought together musical director, voices, production and design in one of the major successes of its performing career ... Richard Bonynge and the Elizabethan Sydney Orchestra began the evening auspiciously on Wednesday with a well-shaped overture. Singing and playing from then on registered Bonynge's direction with a distinctive eloquence and care for detail. The plaintive orchestral phrases in the accompanied recitative for Elvira's "Mi tradi" sang with languishing affection. Overripe? I do not think so.'

The one sad feature of the year was saying farewell to Lone Koppel who was leaving The Australian Opera after several years' residence to return to her home theatre in Copenhagen. Her performances of Jenufa, Jenny in *Mahagonny*, Marie in *Wozzeck*, to mention only a few, were hauntingly memorable. She would return

Above: Joan Sutherland with Dame Margot Fonteyn and Sir Robert Helpmann

occasionally as a guest but never as frequently as one would have liked.

The next new production was *La Traviata* in a grand production designed by Henry Bardon with costumes by Michael Stennett and directed by John Copely. Kiri te Kanawa sang her first Violetta — a role for which she was both vocally and physically suited. Alfredo was Anson Austin, Germont — Robert Allman, Flora — Heather Begg, Annina — Cynthia Johnston, Gaston — Graeme Ewer, the Baron — Pieter van der Stolk, the Marquis — Ronald Maconaghie, and the Doctor — Grant Dickson. This was a very strong cast and Brian Hoad wrote in *The Bulletin* of 'unforgettable moments of music and drama inseparably bound'.

Maria Prerauer in *The Australian* thought it

'superb in every way from its enchanting star Kiri te Kanawa to its simpatico musical direction under Richard Bonynge and John Copley's staging.'

Roger Covell in *The Sydney Morning Herald:*

'Richard Bonynge staked a claim for tragedy, not merely pathos with the nobility of his conducting of the prelude.'

Anson Austin had one of his biggest successes to date and Robert Allman was back in a role that fitted him like a glove. Each of the others in the opera produced telling vignettes and Heather Begg's Flora and Cynthia Johnston's Annina were memorable. We gave seven performances between 21 August and 10 September.

Above: Richard Bonynge acknowledging the orchestra during a dress rehearsal

Apart from the operatic performances of the year most of the principal artists, along with Joan, gave a concert of operatic ensembles similar to the previous year in the Concert Hall and the proceeds were split between the Royal Institute for Deaf and Blind Children and the NSW Friends of the Australian Opera. Joan and I gave a recital for the National Lieder Society on 13 August at the Opera House and I had the temerity to join Ladislav Jasek, Pamela Munks, Irena Morozov and Hans Gyors (our principal string players) in a concert at Chalwin Castle on the shore of the harbour, where we played the Mozart G *minor Quartet*, the Schubert B *flat Trio* and the Schumann *Quintet in E flat*. I felt rather rusty but it was wonderful to play chamber music again — it brought back memories of three idyllic years at the Sydney Conservatorium in the late forties when we spent a whole year playing Haydn trios, another with Mozart and a third with Schubert, Mendelssohn, etc.

The Company was kept exceptionally busy throughout the whole year. They gave concerts in Albury, Wagga-Wagga, Cootamundra, Darwin, Springwood and Parramatta. Two children's operas, *Sid the Serpent who Wanted to Sing* and *Professor Kobalt's Kinetic Kontraption*, were played 258 times in metropolitan and country schools, where they were heard by over 54,000 children. All this in addition to the 211 performances of 21 operas, which says much for the constitutions of most of our singers, many of whom were cruelly overworked.

The year reached a happy conclusion when Her Majesty the Queen created Joan, Dame Commander of the Order of the British Empire.

6
NINETEEN SEVENTY NINE

This was a very busy year with twenty-three operas and a repertoire which included revivals of *Meistersinger*, *Albert Herring*, *Figaro*, *Scarlatti's Triumph of Honour*, *Jenufa*, *Simon Boccanegra*, *Salome*, and new productions of *Fidelio*, *La Fanciulla del West*, *The Abduction from the Seraglio*, *Idomeneo*, *The Queen of Spades*, *Falstaff*, and *Patience*.

The new productions all worked well: *Fanciulla*, conducted by Carlo Felice Cillario, in which Marilyn Zschau made a decided hit; *Falstaff*, a great ensemble piece for the Company, also conducted by Cillario; and *Patience*, with Heather Begg's monstrously funny Lady Jane.

In the Sydney summer season, there was a revival of *Don Giovanni* for four performances, in which the new members of the cast were John Pringle, who sang the Don, Nance Grant — Donna Anna, Margreta Elkins — Elvira, Jennifer Bermingham — Zerlina, and Gregory Yurisich — Masetto. None of these singers resembled their predecessors of last season but they had a well deserved success.

Joan's first operatic appearances in the year were in the February revival of *The Merry Widow* which was played nine times, the major cast change being Beryl Furlan as Valencienne.

The Mirror found Joan in

'beautiful, blissful voice … rather a ripe-looking widow, but she sings gloriously, moves with a stage ease that left some of the established opera singers looking clumsy and topped them all in vocal ease and clarity of dialogue.'

Roger Covell in *The Sydney Morning Herald* wrote:

'She is enchanting, utterly at ease with the part, wholly lovable and genuinely merry … Bonynge's obvious love for the work is reflected in the orchestra's playing and the overall musical control of the evening.'

In November we took *The Merry Widow* production to Adelaide where Ralph Middenway thought it

'one of the most sumptuous productions the country has seen'.

Some critics would have liked to hear Joan in one of her grand opera roles. However,

Facing Page: Joan Sutherland as Violetta. *La Traviata* Act 1

Above: Don Giovanni Act 1. John
Pringle as the Don and Neil Warren-
Smith as Leporello
Right: As Donna Anna in the second
act of *Don Giovanni*

John Kirby decided in *The Sunday Mail*, that

Above: The Merry Widow Act 3

'most opera goers would rather have Sutherland singing the National Anthem instead of no Sutherland at all.'

While in Adelaide, we gave a version of our Opera Concert along with most of the Company, all proceeds going to Channel 10's Childrens' Medical Research Foundation Appeal. We had played this same concert in Sydney on Australia Day (26 January) with all proceeds split three ways between the Royal New South Wales Institute for Deaf and Blind Children, Food for NSW Babies, and the Good Samaritan Associations.

During this year, we made three visits to Melbourne with five performances of

Above: Painting by Michael Stennett of *La Traviata* Act 3. Joan Sutherland and Heather Begg as Violetta and Flora and Robert Allman as Germont

Traviata in March, six *Don Giovannis* in August and six *Merry Widows* in December. The critics were rather hostile but the public was welcoming.

Because of its capacity Joan was always put into the old Palais in St Kilda. This theatre, which was built in 1913 as the Palais de Danse Picture Theatre, is still the largest in Australia, seating above three thousand. Its acoustics are good but its back-stage accommodation was stinking; and I use the word intentionally. It is situated right next to a fair ground and one Saturday night the last act of *Traviata* seemed to gain in reality from the fair noises heard outside Violetta's sickroom. We enjoyed our visit to Melbourne for which we have always had an inordinate affection ever since our 1965 tour.

James Morris came with us to Melbourne to sing Don Giovanni to Joan's Anna. Margreta Elkins was Elvira, Kathleen Moore — Zerlina, Henri Wilden — Ottavio, Neil Warren-Smith — Leporello, Clifford Grant — the Commendatore and Lyndon Terracini — Masetto.

At the end of March, we went to Brisbane for four performances of *Norma*. Val Vallis wrote in *The Australian:*

'It is fourteen years since Joan Sutherland last sang in Brisbane and over 60 years since the Gonzalez Opera Company presented the last *Norma* here. Sutherland has never sounded better.'

Above: Flora (Heather Begg) and the ballet in *La Traviata*
Left: La Traviata last act with Anson Austin as Alfredo

Top: Die Entführung Act II Finale. (From left) Glenys Fowles (Constanze), Paul Ferris (Belmonte), Pieter van der Stolk (Pasha Selim), Anson Austin (Pedrillo) and Rhonda Bruce (Blonde) *Above: Die Entführung* Paul Ferris as Belmonte

Norma's two children were local performers and one of them made his presence felt during 'Mira, o Norma' by playing trains on the set, choo-chooing loudly about the stage, until Beryl Furlan (singing Clotilde) dragged him off by the scruff of the neck. Brisbane had changed enormously since 1965 and we enjoyed being there with Margreta Elkins (Adalgisa) back in her own town and with Ronald Stevens and Clifford Grant in the cast.

My first opera in the Sydney winter season was a revival of the previous year's *Traviata* for four performances with Joan Carden as Violetta, Henri Wilden as Alfredo and Gregory Yurisich as Germont. I believe all these artists were singing the roles for the first time.

Following *Traviata*, I conducted performances of a revival of Mozart's *Die Entführung aus dem Serail* which had previously been given in English as *The Abduction from the Seraglio*. This of course gave some of the critics something to gripe about — whatever the language, someone would complain. Michael Beauchamp reproduced George Ogilvie's original production. It was called a 'revival' although the sets were entirely new as a warehouse fire the previous year had claimed the first lot. Glenys Fowles sang Constanze, Paul Ferris — Belmonte, Rhonda Bruce — Blonde, Anson Austin — Pedrillo, and Donald Shanks — Osmin. This was a well-balanced cast topped off by Pieter van der Stolk's extraordinarily powerful performance of the Pasha Selim, a speaking role which so often goes for nothing.

Nadine Amadio thought it 'a stylish new *Seraglio*, marked by a mercurial grace' and Maria Prerauer described it as 'full of pace, colour and bounce'.

This year was a feast of Mozart as our next new production was *Idomeneo*, which the Company had bought from the Victorian State Opera. This was designed by John Truscott and produced by Robin Lovejoy, and we played seven performances. Leona Mitchell sang her first Ilia, Joan her first Elettra, and in fact the entire cast sang their roles for the first time. Margreta Elkins sang Idamante (with the glorious aria 'Non temer amato bene' which Mozart added for the Vienna revival); Ronald Stevens and Sergei Baigildin both sang Idomeneo.

At one of the performances both our tenors fell seriously ill and a third Idomeneo

Above: Die Entführung aus dem Serail
Act 3. (Left to right) Anson Austin
(Pedrillo), Rhonda Bruce (Blonde),
Glenys Fowles (Constanze) and Paul
Ferris (Belmonte)
Left: Die Entführung Donald Shanks as
Osmin and Anson Austin as Pedrillo

Above: Idomeneo. Joan Sutherland as Elettra in Act 1
Above Centre: Idomeneo Leona Mitchell as Ilia
Above Right: Idomeneo Margreta Elkins as Idamante

ready to sing the role we did not have, so the *Traviata* sets were dragged out of the warehouse at the last possible moment. Without any rehearsal on anybody's part, we all got up and performed one of the best *Traviatas* we ever did in Sydney — if not the best. The atmosphere was electric and everybody was on his toes. The cast was the same for the Melbourne performances earlier in the year, but for Sydney audiences it was Joan's first appearance in this production and her only one in the current season.

Roger Covell described the performance as

'full of vocal elation and dramatic excitement ... the Company's work came together with exceptional decisiveness and urgency. Sutherland sang with phenomenal accuracy and brilliance ... her partners (Anson Austin and Roger Allman) responded memorably to the challenge of the occasion ... Richard Bonynge's direction was full of character and strength. The evening was a personal triumph for him.'

As well as praising Anson Austin and Robert Allman, Maria Prerauer wrote of Joan that she

'sang like some angelic visitation from on high. She could scarcely have been more impressive or unleashed if she had been preparing for a month.'

The Chairman of The Australian Opera, Mr Charles Berg, announced on Wednesday, 24 October that The Australian Opera had approached Mr Kenneth Tribe, asking him to act in an interim capacity as Management Co-ordinator and that Mr Tribe has agreed to do so. On 18 October, Mr Berg released the following statement:

'An agreement has been reached between The Australian Opera and Mr Peter Hemmings as to the termination of his engagement as General Manager as of today. The terms have been mutually agreed by the parties. Neither party wishes to make any further statement on the matter.'

This bland statement concealed a lot of backstage shilly-shallying. Some of it had to do with my disagreements with Mr Hemmings, but more was to do with his relations with the Board and financial matters. The whole Company experienced a

couple of unpleasant weeks, most of which I thankfully and expediently forgot. The result was that Mr Hemmings was no more in Australia.

During this year the Joan Sutherland Society was formed, with Lady Braddon and the Earl of Harewood as patrons. It was founded by a group of admirers with the aim of assisting operatic talent in the community, and is still continuing its work to good effect. We have a jolly dinner with them from time to time.

A *This is your Life* on television was a surprise for Joan on 14 March. Our old friends Margreta Elkins, Terry McEwen, Russell Braddon and Norman Ayrton were flown in for it and Marilyn Horne, Luciano Pavarotti and Franco Zeffirelli all made appearances. The world premiere of Brian Adams' 80 minute film documentary *A Life on the Move*, which showed our gypsy-like existence, took place at the Everest Theatre in the Seymour Centre, Sydney, on 26 July.

A record of Mozart arias and duets which Isobel Buchanan, John Pringle and I made with the Queensland Symphony Orchestra, was issued and remains a splendid souvenir of these fine artists.

In an already overbusy year four of our singers went on a trek, giving concerts in Cairns, Rockhampton, Townsville, Armidale, Tamworth, Lismore and other towns off the operatic beat.

Montserrat Caballé visited Sydney, Adelaide and Melbourne for three concerts and Australia was richer for hearing this enchanting artist.

Majorie Lawrence, Australia's most courageous singer, died this year, aged 71. We had heard her in the forties in Sydney and she came to our performances both in Italy and America. After being struck by polio in 1941 she continued her career, mostly from a wheelchair for many years. She is remembered with love by her many fans and students and makes us aware of the impermanence of our careers.

Tchaikovsky's *Queen of Spades* opened in Sydney on 18 July — we gave seven performances, then opened the Adelaide November season with four more, and the following month in Melbourne with a further three. The production itself and the sets were not universally admired by the Press. Arbit Blatas sent models of the sets, and in transferring these models to the stage something went wrong. I think it was the usual matter of finance and of some lack of communication between the theatre and Mr Blatas, who is an artist of high reputation and much in demand. The Australian Opera's workshops are capable of producing superb work but I think this was the nadir of their efforts. There was a lot of interference from someone who would have

Above Top: Gregory Dempsey as
Ghermann and Rosina Raisbeck as the
Countess in Act 2 Scene 2 of *The
Queens of Spades*
Above: Marilyn Richardson as Lisa in
the *Queen of Spades* Act 3 Scene 2

been better minding his own business. For my part, I more than enjoyed working
with Regina Resnik as producer. Her years of experience on stage, her complete
understanding of her craft and ability to transfer her ideas and teach them technical-
ly made her an ideal person to work with our Company and this work benefitted our
more intelligent singers. The Press was, as usual, divided about language and had a
field-day with atrocious puns about trumps, but I think Tchaikovsky won in the end.
The cast was evenly matched and sang and performed the opera well. Gregory
Dempsey was Ghermann, Marilyn Richardson — Lisa, Rosina Raisbeck — the
Countess (Regina Resnik sang the last three), John Pringle was Tomsky, Gregory
Yurisich — Yeletsky, Etela Piha — Pauline, Cynthia Johnston and Kathleen Moore
— the Governess, Angela Denning — Chloe, and Robert Gard/John Serge, Bruce
Martin, Erik Badcock/Anthony Clark, and Robert Eddie the four officers.

'*The Queen of Spades* opened with a memorable torrent of orchestra sound,' wrote
John Sinclair in *The Melbourne Herald*.

'In playing the intense doom-laden prelude to this splendid opera, the Elizabethan
Sydney Orchestra under Richard Bonynge's ardent and authoritative direction produced
the richest and most balanced tone I have heard in any operatic performance this season.'

Roger Covell in *The Sydney Morning* Herald expressed

'gratitude for the inclusion of Tchaikovsky's masterly opera in the current Australian
Opera repertory ... Richard Bonynge's conducting, expressive of a deep love of the work,

was answered by some fine solo singing … and a well-pointed, urgently-paced account of
the overwhelming riches of Tchaikovsky's orchestral writing.'

Above: The Queen of Spades Set design
by Arbit Blatas for Act 2 Scene 2

Kenneth Hince in *The Age* thought it

'a night's experience which is always absorbing, sometimes compelling — deeply reso-
nant, vibrant with colour, and with the instrumental solos clear as the morning star.'

He considered that Marilyn Richardson gave a performance of 'outstanding dig-
nity and beauty' as Lisa.

What a great opera it is. Nine years elapsed before I had the pleasure of conducting
it again.

7

NINETEEN EIGHTY

This year brought with it a few changes. Since Mr Hemmings' departure, Ken Tribe had acted as General Manager and generally kept the peace while the Board searched for a new incumbent. Their first choice seemed to be Miss Ardis Krainik, Assistant General Manager of the Lyric Opera, Chicago, but the Board shilly-shallied so long that the good lady sensibly accepted the far more remunerative, and undoubtedly calmer position of General Manager of her own opera company at the resignation of Carol Fox.

The Board's next choice was Patrick Veitch, who was working in the Metropolitan Opera's marketing department. So Mr Veitch and his wife, Kathleen Norris, arrived with, we all hoped, some American financial expertise to stabilise our shaky economy — shaky, I might add, because of miserable governmental support, not because of the box office.

During this year we gave 219 performances of 21 productions in five cities. There were 293,976 paid attendances and an average of over 80 per cent attendance at the box office. The repertoire consisted of Scarlatti's *Triumph of Honour*, a new production of Walton's *The Bear, The Pearl Fishers* (borrowed for a season from the Victorian State Opera), *Patience, Lucia* (new), *The Magic Flute, Nabucco, La Fanciulla del West, Don Giovanni, La Traviata, Falstaff, The Abduction from the Seraglio, Les Contes d'Hoffman, Manon Lescaut* (new), Verdi's *I Masnadieri* (new), *Rigoletto, Il Barbiere di Siviglia, Fra Diavolo, Boris Godunov* (new), *A Midsummer Night's Dream*, and *Katya Kabanova* (new).

Lucia was the opera the audiences had been demanding for some time and a splendid production by John Copley was mounted with sets by Henry Bardon and costumes by Michael Stennett, all in the rather lovely acoustic environment of the much more ample Concert Hall. This Concert Hall was originally intended by the architect, Joern Utzon, as the Opera House, but in those days the Australian Broadcasting Commission, which was then more politically powerful than The Australian Opera, usurped it for their own use and several million pounds worth of stage machinery was dumped in a field to rust. It is to be hoped that one day the Opera will steal the hall right back.

Lucia was a resounding success and we played twenty-two performances during the year: eight in the Sydney summer season, six in the winter, four in Adelaide, and four in the Melbourne Palais.

The cast included Richard Greager as Edgardo (Paul Ferris and Lamberto Furlan

Facing Page: Costume design for Joan Sutherland in *I Masnadieri* Act 2, by Michael Stennett

Above: The Magic Flute John Pringle as
Papageno
Right: The Magic Flute Isobel Buchanan
as Pamina and Graeme Ewer as
Monostatos

in Melbourne), Robert Allman and Erik Badcock as Enrico, Clifford Grant as
Raimondo (Donald Shanks in Melbourne), Rosina Raisbeck as Alisa, Henri Wilden
as Arturo and Robin Donald as Normanno.

So much has been written elsewhere about *Lucia* that I will use the space to deal
with some of the lesser-known operas. But members of the Press were universally
kind, not to say euphoric and hyperbolic, and it was rather nicely summed up by W.L.
Hoffmann in *The Canberra Times*:

> 'Every once in a while there comes a musical performance so outstanding that one knows
> instinctively that it will remain forever in the memory, one of those touchstones of
> experience that subsequently will be referred to whenever one is seeking a gauge of
> excellence.'

Brian Hoad in *The Bulletin* brings us a vivid picture:

> 'What always was, and still is, a miracle is the way she brings the poor mad thing alive —

the waves of torment and dementia that fluctuate through her face, the wild eyes, the crazy smiles, the flutterings and staggerings, the final heart-stopping collapse. It is here that Sutherland, with supreme artistic skill, reaches out and touches her audience's heart in a way that nobody else can quite match. It is the piece of total theatrical magic on which her legend was founded.'

Above: Painting by Michael Stennett of the Wedding Scene in *Lucia di Lammermoor* with Robert Allman as Enrico, Joan Sutherland as Lucia and Henri Wilden as Arturo

During the performances of Mad Lucy, I kept my sanity with six *Magic Flutes* in February-March and another five in August-September. Glenys Fowles, Lynne Cantlon and Isobel Buchanan sang Pamina, Anson Austin and Robin Donald — Tamino, John Pringle and John Fulford — Papageno, Rhonda Bruce — the Queen, Neil Warren-Smith — Sarastro, Etela Piha/Beryl Furlan, Kathleen Moore and Rosemary Gunn — the Three Ladies, Bruce Martin — the Speaker, Graeme Ewer — Monostatos, and Cynthia Johnston — Papagena.

'Revived for the umpteenth time,' wrote Fred Blanks in *The Sydney Morning Herald*, 'this hardy survivor of the unforgettable 1973 Opera House production shows few signs of approaching its expiry date.' Both Glenys Fowles and Isobel Buchanan were highly praised, as was John Fulford playing Papageno for the first time. Continued Mr Blanks:

'Neil Warren-Smith's Sarastro, Cynthia Johnston's Papagena, John Stoddart's costumes and Richard Bonynge's conducting all remain enduring successes. So does this whole *Magic Flute*. The final winner is Mozart.'

Above Top: Lucia di Lammermoor Act 1 Scene 2. Joan Sutherland as Lucia
Above: Rigoletto Joan Carden and Raymond Myers as Gilda and Rigoletto
Right: Lucia di Lammermoor Act 2 Scene 1. Robert Allman as Enrico and Joan Sutherland as Lucia

We gave the Australian première of *I Masnadieri* on 2 July and played the opera eleven times during the winter season. This was the only opera which Verdi wrote for London and the role of the heroine, Amalia, was written for Jenny Lind. Peter Beauvais directed, with sets by Allan Lees and costumes by Michael Stennett.

There was some excitement, as this was the first time that Joan and Donald Smith, Australia's premier tenor of the sixties and seventies, were to sing together in opera. He had the weight and quality of voice of a true Verdi tenor and sang the role wonderfully throughout rehearsal. Unfortunately he barely completed two performances when he fell severely ill. Paul Ferris courageously completed the run in a role which was undoubtedly heavy for him but he handled it with expertise. Robert Allman had a great success as the villainous Francesco and the cast further consisted of Clifford Grant in a very congenial role as Massimiliano, Bruce Martin as Moser, making an important part out of a small one, Lamberto Furlan as Arminio, and Erik Badcock as Rolla.

W.L. Hoffmann pointed out in *The Canberra Times* that this was the first time that Joan had made her début in a major role in Australia (he probably did not count *Suor Angelica*, as it is only one act). He wrote:

'The special qualities which Verdi wrote into the role of Amalia for Jenny Lind particu-larly suit Joan Sutherland's voice, and she was right at the top of her form. Her first aria, 'Lo squardo avea degli angeli', was sung with such refinement, ease and beauty as to stir the audience into an enthusiastic response, a reaction which was repeated many times during the evening ... Richard Bonynge conducted, with excellent control of the musi-cal disparity between the first two acts, which are typical early-Verdi, and the final acts which look forward to his later style. He obtained fine playing from the Elizabethan Trust Orchestra — the ovation that he received individually at the end, showed that Sydney opera goers at least recognise the musical quality he has brought to The Australian Opera as its Musical Director over the past four years.'

Above: Fra Diavolo Act 1. Heather Begg and Gordon Wilcock as Lord and Lady Allcash

Brian Hoad wrote in *The Bulletin:*

'On stage the Company brought out its biggest guns. Joan Sutherland, Donald Smith, Robert Allman and Clifford Grant would be difficult to upstage in a recital of nursery rhymes. In a thumpingly good piece of early Verdi they were unbeatable ... *I Masnadieri,* under the strong direction of Richard Bonynge in the pit, provides a solidly satisfying evening of operatic thrills and spills. It's a rediscovery of which the rest of the operatic world is probably going to hear much more.'

Opera Australia reported that 'at the end of the performance thousands of gold and yellow chrysanthemum petals showered upon the stage as the performers were greet-ed by the stamping, applauding, capacity audience.'
This opera was revived again in 1981 and 1987.
The winter season this year turned into quite a marathon as far as I was concerned, and I found myself for several weeks on end conducting five performances as well as

Above: Fra Diavolo Act 1. Angela Denning as Zerlina and Pieter van der Stolk as the Innkeeper

the necessary rehearsals. Although blessed with a strong constitution, I confess that I was fairly tired at the end of my stay.

In between the *Masnadieri* performances there were nine *Rigolettos,* with Joan Carden an exquisitely musical Gilda, Raymond Myers — Rigoletto, Anson Austin — the Duke, Bruce Martin — Monterone, Donald Shanks as Sparafucile, and Heather Begg as Maddalena. We toured it to Melbourne in the Palais with the same cast except for Reginald Byers as the Duke and Lesley Stender as Maddalena. This was the same production we did in Wellington in 1976 and it is still being revived.

Just before leaving Sydney for a few months, I conducted the first two performances of a revival of *Fra Diavolo* with a substantially different cast from the 1977 performances. Angela Denning sang Zerlina, Anson Austin, who had before sung Lorenzo, sang Diavolo, and Paul Ferris sang Lorenzo. Heather Begg repeated her old role, with Gordon Wilcock as Lord Allcash. Graeme Ewer remained as Beppo, with John Germain this time as Giacomo and Pieter van der Stolk as Matteo.

'Occasionally the froth on top of our opera glasses,' wrote Fred Blanks in *The Sydney Morning Herald,* 'is more refreshing than some of the murky material beneath. A case in point is *Fra Diavolo,* the comic opera by Auber which returned, chuckling all the way, to The Australian Opera repertoire on Thursday evening.' He thought Heather Begg 'terrifyingly amourous', that Anson Austin 'swashbuckles nicely' and that I kept it 'all sizzling'.

Adrian Read in *The Daily Telegraph* thought Anson Austin

'sings the role strongly and looks devilishly handsome'

and that Angela Denning, in her first major role for The Australian Opera,

'looked perfect, acted with flair and handled the vocal acrobatics with sufficient skill to make it certain we'll be seeing and hearing a great deal more of her.'

Above: Fra Diavolo Act 1. Heather Begg (Lady Pamela) and Anson Austin (Fra Diavolo)

In fact, Angela has sung many major roles at the Deutsche Oper in Berlin and had a big success as Queen Marguerite in their production of Meyerbeer's *Les Huguenots*. She was recently singing at the Salzburg Festival.

I remember with relish the opening night of *Boris Godonov* in Adelaide. Joan and I went along because we had so enjoyed the production in Sydney. There was a major and unforeseen difference. It was deemed impractical to transport the fowls used in the Inn Scene from Sydney to Adelaide, and the local poultry, making their débuts, were far less theatrical birds. In fact they kicked up an almighty ruckus during rehearsals so it was decided to sedate them. The sedative obviously had too strong an effect and when they were thrown through the window upstage they landed with a clunk like bags of cement. Halfway into the scene they began to show signs of life. Whenever tenor Gordon Wilcock sang, they squawked along. As the drug wore off they became more unruly and were all over the stage. Gordon Wilcock, singing Missail, gave one of them a kick out of his way and all hell broke loose — there were fowls everywhere creating a fearful racket! Two of them flew off the stage into the pit — one landed on the head of the first horn, who didn't miss a note, and the other at the foot of the conductor, Peter Seymour, where it lay rather dazed. At the end of the act Peter left the pit carrying off his prize. I doubt the scene was ever applauded so vociferously.

The year in general was so busy and so enjoyable that one hardly noticed the constant quarrels with regard to funding — the constant meetings and conferences with all those who had nothing whatever to do with the work in hand having too much say. I did the best I could to make my rehearsals coincide with their palaver.

8

NINETEEN EIGHTY ONE

Although this was a year of rising costs, and reduced grants, when most companies throughout the world were feeling the pinch, The Australian Opera managed to give a season of 21 operas (or 23 if one includes concert performances of *Die Walküre* and *Götterdämmerung*) of which seven were new productions.

We revived Britten's *Rape of Lucretia* and *Midsummer Night's Dream*, Mozart's *Don Giovanni* and *Figaro*, Verdi's *Rigoletto*, *Traviata*, *Macbeth*, and *I Masnadieri*, Janacek's *Jenufa* and *Katya Kabanova*; *Bohème*, *Manon Lescaut*, *Hoffmann* and *The Barber of Seville*. The new productions were *Otello*, *The Beggar's Opera*, Handel's *Alcina*, Meyerbeer's *Les Huguenots*, Piccinni's *La Buona Figliuola*, Puccini's *Tosca*, and Smetana's *The Bartered Bride*.

Otello was Joan's first opera for the year, in a splendid production by George Ogilvie with costumes by Kristian Fredrikson. This played for ten performances in the Concert Hall of the Sydney Opera House during January and February, and a further six in the Melbourne Palais in May/June. Angelo Marenzi sang Otello, and John Shaw (Sydney) and Robert Allman (Melbourne) — Iago. Emilia was shared between Heather Begg and Kathleen Moore, Lodovico between Clifford Grant and Donald Shanks. Cassio was sung by Paul Ferris, Roderigo by Robin Donald and Montano by Bruce Martin and John Wegner. Carlo Felice Cillario conducted all the performances. He has done more, musically, for The Australian Opera than any other conductor and has given his time generously to our singers and orchestras for many years, and continues to do so. Joan was very happy singing Desdemona with him and judging by the seraphic smiles from the pit it was a mutual feeling. Carlo has quite a sense of humour. He offered to conduct *I Pagliacci* for nothing provided the Company paid him double for *Cavalleria Rusticana*.

Thomas Schick in *The Australian Art News* praised Joan's

> 'surprisingly full and ripe lower notes. With her, not for a moment does one feel that something is there simply for effect, without motivation ... there is never anything sham, or showy or attention seeking ... Her portrayal is a musical crescendo that moves from a rather bland Act 1 to a subtle delineation of Desdemona's inherent submissiveness and "femininity" in Act 2, to the magnificent outpouring of despair in the big ensemble scene that crowns Act 3, and finally to the climactic full-voiced closing moments of the "Willow Song" ... Desdemona is not the most gratifying role in Sutherland's career, but there is no doubt that seeing her, one is seeing a great artist.'

Facing Page: Portrait in oils of Joan Sutherland as Violetta in first act of *La Traviata* by Michael Stennett

Above: The Beggar's Opera Act 2.
Jennifer Bermingham as Dolly Trull and
John Pringle as Macheath
Right: The Beggar's Opera Act 2. John
Germain as Lockit, Rosina Raisbeck as
Mrs Trapes, and Gordon Wilcock as
Peacham

John Sinclair wrote in *The Melbourne Herald* that

> 'her singing last night throughout the great final act is something that I will long remember. As I will the soaring legato line she sustained in the quartet in Act 2.'

Maria Prerauer in *The Australian* found Joan

> 'in glorious soaring voice as Desdemona … (This) proved what many have long suspected: that she can be just as stunning in noble lyric soprano roles like this as in the silly potboilers she usually favours.'

I suppose by 'silly potboilers' Mrs Prerauer means *Lucia, Puritani, Norma, Semiramide, Traviata, Don Giovanni* et al — these being the ones Joan favours.

A concurrent effort in the season was a new version of *The Beggar's Opera* which Douglas Gamley and I worked out together. I had plenty of ideas but it was Douglas who did the bulk of the work and his orchestrations were very amusing and brilliant. The piece was conceived quite simply as a popular entertainment — a musical. More specifically, it showed Hollywood in the thirties making a film of *The Beggar's Opera*. The Press was quite divided — many missed the point entirely and others, if they saw the joke, were, like Queen Victoria, not amused.

The open dress rehearsal had a phenomenal success with the public and perhaps because of this the first night seemed rather down — but that was only momentary. We played it ten times in Sydney during February and eight times at the lovely Princess Theatre, Melbourne, in May.

Anthony Besch wrote an amusing book and John Stoddart did some marvellous costumes and sets. Half of the Company took part in this romp and appeared to enjoy

themselves and certainly allowed the public a good time. Macheath was played by John Pringle, Polly Peachum by Anne-Maree McDonald, Lucy Lockit by Lynne Cantlon and Angela Denning. Mrs Peachum was sung by Heather Begg and Peachum by Gordon Wilcock, Lockit by John Germain, Filch by Graeme Ewer, and Mrs Trapes by Rosina Raisbeck. The ladies of the town were Cynthia Johnston, Lesley Stender, Lois Empey, Judith Saliba, Elizabeth Fretwell, Jennifer Bermingham and Beryl Furlan. Jemmy Twitcher was played by Erik Badcock and Matt of the Mint by Ronald Stevens. Anthony Warlow was the scriptwriter, John Gay, and Messrs Strohberg and Reich, a pair of Hollywood moguls, were played by Ronald Stevens and Robert Eddie.

W.L. Hoffmann in *The Canberra Times* found it

> 'a lively, amusing production which brings much of the parodistic-satirical element of Gay's original into line with the twentieth century ... in setting it within the trappings of a Hollywood film musical of the 1930s, Bonynge and Gamley have given it a new twist and taken full advantage of the possibilities of musical parody which the framework offers. Amusing musical quotations and parodies crop up all through — from Handel to Stephen Sondheim — and Gamley's scoring (for a large orchestra of course) is so much in the vein of Hollywood's highly-coloured over treatment of its big musicals that it adds its own incongruities for the amusement of the listener ... In contrast to Gay's original, which was written for actors rather than singers, this new version calls for singers of quality, with some roles quite demanding vocally ... The orchestra under Bonynge's direction made some lovely, lush "Hollywood orchestra" sounds and carried off the ragtime parodies well ... This is not a serious presentation, and perhaps that is what upset the Sydney critics (they take their opera so seriously), but I found it a diverting and entertaining production, just the right thing for a summer season.'

Kenneth Hince in the Melbourne *Age* wrote

> 'Douglas Gamley's orchestration struck me as a simple and very expert piece of updating,

Right: The Beggar's Opera Prologue.
Ronald Stevens as Mr Strohberg, Robert
Eddie as Mr Reich, and Anthony
Warlow as John Gay

with an occasional mordant note reminiscent of Walton or Stravinsky in their handling
of older music ... It was extremely well handled by Bonynge, who managed in some mys-
terious way to draw quite a decent sound out of the orchestra even at the Princess Theatre
... I enjoyed the performance very much as a good-natured romp ... John Stoddart's stage
designs were amusing and practical, and the Besch-Bremner production kept the action
tactfully balanced inside the suggested framework of the film studio. This conceit could
have been a disaster if clumsily handled, but was in fact treated with fine judgement ...
As a performance it made an excellent coda to the Melbourne season.'

In the *Australian Art News* Thomas Schick wrote

'It is a well-oiled, superb-to-look-at production in which the members of The Australian
Opera show what accomplished comics and comediennes they can be if need be. In fact it
would be unfair to single anyone out. There was no weak link in their comic contribu-
tions, or in the visual and directorial ingenuity which surrounded them. Under Richard
Bonynge's direction the Sydney Elizabethan Orchestra played with great sheen.'

Nadine Amadio in *The Sydney Telegraph*:

'*The Beggar's Opera* in Hollywood has come to the Opera House and the audience love it.
So they should. It's great entertainment and as a showpiece for The Australian Opera
cast it underlines their extreme professionalism ... This time it has been

"Hollywoodised" and why not send up Tinsel City? It's as good a way of mocking man's vanity as satirising politicians or art trends.'

It was all a fine piece of frivolity for us in the midst of the lugubrious tragedies which we were wont to perform night after night.

Another tragedy, and one of the greatest, was to be our first opera for the Sydney winter season in June/July. We gave seven *Traviatas* with Richard Greager as Alfredo, Jonathan Summers as Germont, Rosemary Gunn as Flora, and the stalwarts of the Company in their wonted roles. 'The night was Dame Joan's, Dame Joan's and Dame Joan's again,' wrote Maria Prerauer in *The Australian:*

'La Stupenda turned her appearance ... in the title role of *La Traviata* — Verdi's most intimate and lovely work — into yet another great personal triumph ... The cheers after Dame Joan's clutch of florid first act arias, complete with a couple of new twists to the coloraturas, could surely have been heard halfway across Sydney harbour ... If Dame Joan

Above: Otello Act 1. Joan Sutherland
(Desdemona) with Angelo Marenzi
(Otello)

seemed to have just a little too much of what the Victorians called "a fine figure of a woman" to be wholly believable as a consumptive courtesan fading to a shadow before one's eyes, it didn't seem to matter a crotchet. All Sutherland has to do to enchant an audience is to stand there and open her mouth and let those radiant tones stream out — rich, creamy, velvet and wholly unique in quality. So compelling is the legendary magic of her magnificent soprano that she can still bring down the house by the sheer impact of her singing alone.'

W.L. Hoffmann wrote:

Above: Otello Act 3 with Angelo
Marenzi (Otello)

'Her first phrase at the opening of the first act "Flora, amici, la notte che resta" is not particularly notable musically but it was so beautifully phrased and such a magnificent sound
that the impact on the audience was almost physical. In the periods between hearing it
one tends to forget the power, beauty and flexibility of that VOICE; each time one hears
it again there is an initial reaction of excitement and pleasure, mixed with some
incredulity ... her "Follie! Follie!" which concludes the act was a display of vocal virtuosity which almost brought the house down. The amazing thing is that each time one hears
Sutherland singing of late she seems to be singing even better; there is no sense of
holding back or of nursing her vocal resources through a performance. It is fully

committed singing right throughout … vocally there is surely no other soprano in the world to match her … I sat entranced from beginning to end — it was assuredly a performance to remember.'

Nadine Amadio wrote:

'She is one of the few sopranos today who can bring a real excitement to the coloratura aria like "Sempre libera" and yet have the richness and warmth to convey the impact of the more tender passages. Looking amazingly youthful, her performance was one of great substance and radiance.'

Above: La Traviata Act 4. with Richard Greager as Alfredo

The new production of Handel's *Alcina* was the first work I had done with Sir Robert Helpmann, who brought all his theatrical flair and knowledge to work on this old masterpiece. The sets and costumes by John Pascoe were among the most beautiful ever seen on the Australian stage. The Press, which in Australia is very money-conscious, complained of the cost — the extravagance — but I believe it was worth it. In any case, the approximately two hundred thousand dollars which it cost was a flea-bite compared to the millions of dollars spent by the Metropolitan Opera or La Scala on one production.

John Connolly said in *The National Times:*

'The Australian Opera has taken a long-overdue step by finally offering its audiences a large-scale baroque opera, Handel's masterpiece, *Alcina* … the quality of the music in *Alcina* is so high and the standard of the singing is such that no true music lover could resist it.'

The Sun Herald called it

'a super show (forget it is an opera) of incredible splendour, costumes wildly ornate and beautiful, gorgeous scenes changing before one's eyes as in a pantomime transformation, arias of lilting extravagance and a plot so unreal there was no need to follow it.'

David Vance, in the same newspaper, wrote

'Handel's brilliant music is dazzling in both its invention and beauty: it is multifaceted — now virtuosic, now elegantly simple, always appealing. Richard Bonynge maintained a brisk pace throughout but one which always allowed the singers space to polish their individual jewels of arias to a high degree. Joan Carden as Alcina and Margreta Elkins as Ruggiero were both marvellous. Do not miss this production.'

In addition to these ladies the cast included Heather Begg as Bradamante, Angela Denning and Beryl Furlan as Morgana, Anne-Maree McDonald as Oberto, Paul Ferris as Oronte and Donald Shanks as Melisso.

Opera seria, being new to Sydney, prompted Roger Covell to write:

'It will hold them, I believe, by the power, beauty and inexhaustible variety of Handel's score and the simple, though far from inexpensive, pleasure to be had from John Pascoe's designs. Richard Bonynge conducts with lively affection, the singers make a brisk and mostly handsome sound … and the perspective sets, with their exuberant, theatrically baroque architecture, are a delight.'

John Cargher in *The Age* had this to say:

'The Australian Ballet should not have allowed Sir Robert Helpmann to leave. Any producer capable of making a high-grade popular entertainment out of a Handel opera is nothing short of a genius.'

Above: La Traviata Act 3 (Left to right) John Germain as the Marquis, Heather Begg as Flora, Joan Sutherland as Violetta and Graeme Ewer as Gaston

And *The Telegraph:*

'In spite of the superb singing, the real stars of this production are conductor Richard Bonynge, about two dozen brilliant performing musicians and a magnificent little lady called Sharolyn Kimmorley, who spins her harpsichord magic ceaselessly throughout the evening.'

We played *Alcina* twelve times in July/August and it has already had two successful revivals.

After *Alcina* we launched into Meyerbeer's spectacular *Les Huguenots,* a type of grand opera not seen in Australia this century. John Stoddart created magnificent sets but for financial reasons these were cut down considerably and what we were left with, while looking good, was only half of his conception. Michael Stennett's cos-

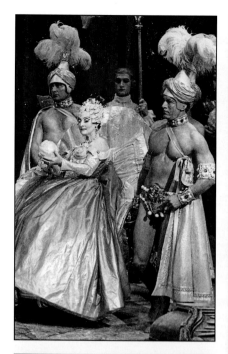

Above Top: *Alcina* Heather Begg as
Bradamante
Above: *Alcina* Act 1. Alcina (Joan
Carden) with her bodyguard
Right: *Alcina* Joan Carden as Alcina and
Margreta Elkins as Ruggiero

tumes were among his most brilliant and here no expense was spared. Lotfi Mansouri
directed this huge warhorse on the small stage of the Opera House with forceful dramatic impact.

The opera critic for *The Canberra Times* had this to say:

'The Australian Opera is to be commended for undertaking the first production of a big
Meyerbeer opera in this country and so providing audiences with a wider experience
than the general repertoire.'

But Maria Prerauer in *The Australian* was quite cross:

'For the money squandered on this superseded Victorian monstrosity The Australian
Opera could have staged at least one Wagner *Ring* cycle music drama or *Tristan and Isolde*
or *Parsifal*, or Strauss's *Elektra*.'

George Kennedy in *The Sun* thought

'*Les Huguenots* is a major step in the history of The Australian Opera … *Les Huguenots*
has been dubbed "The Night of the Seven Stars" for the quantity of principal artists needed to sustain it, and The Australian Opera provided them with honours … Friday's opening performance is a remarkable achievement.'

Brian Hoad in *The Bulletin:*

'The pleasures of the evening are mainly musical. The chorus, getting its big break of the
season, makes the most of the great choral outbursts which punctuate the opera. Richard

Bonynge and the band work up complementary outbursts of excitement in the pit ... The singing, often excruciatingly difficult, is uniformly a delight. Sutherland is vocally immaculate and splendidly imperious ... *Les Huguenots* is an apt gesture on the part of the Company, on the occasion of its 25th Anniversary, to show just how far it has progressed musically.

W.L. Hoffmann wrote:

Above Top: Les Huguenots Act 2. (Front right to left) Anson Austin (Raoul), Joan Sutherland (Queen Marguerite), Bruce Martin (St Bris), Beryl Furlan (First Lady of Honour), John Pringle (Nevers), Marilyn Zschau (Valentine) and Rosemary Gunn (Second Lady of Honour) *Above: Les Huguenots* Final scene. Bruce Martin as St Bris

Right Top: Les Huguenots Act 1. Ronald
Stevens as Cossé and Anson Austin as
Raoul
Right Below: Les Huguenots Act 3 The
Fight

'Joan Sutherland brings authority and stature to the central role of Marguerite de Valois,
revelling in the vocal acrobatics with the greatest brilliance and assurance ... Richard
Bonynge conducted with his usual firm control of both singers and orchestra and maintained this strong musical direction throughout the long four hours of the opera.'

The mammoth cast included Marilyn Zschau as Valentine, Anne-Maree
McDonald and Judith Saliba as the Page, Anson Austin and Richard Greager as
Raoul, John Pringle as Nevers, Bruce Martin as St Bris and Clifford Grant as Marcel.
One of the opera's strengths was the fine work of so many of our singers in the smaller
roles. The Catholic gentlemen were played by Paul Ferris as Tavannes, Don Lister as
Thoré, Gregory Yurisich as de Retz, Ronald Stevens or Robin Donald as Cossé and
John Fulford as Méru. Marguerite's ladies of honour were sung by Beryl Furlan and
Rosemary Gunn, and the two young girls by Angela Denning and Judith Saliba or
Helen Borthwick, and the gypsies by Elizabeth Fretwell or Nicola Waite, and Leslie
Stender or Kathleen Moore. The Nightwatchman was Erik Badcock, Bois-Rose was
Serge Baigildin and the three monks, John Antoniou, Robert Eddie and John
Durham. The *Corps de ballet* was led by Lois Strike and Serge Volobuyev.

I will let Roger Covell in *The Sydney Morning Herald* have the last word:

'It takes some considerable time for The Australian Opera's new production of *Les*

Left: *Les Huguenots* Act 4 Valentine (Marilyn Zschau) and Raoul (Anson Austin)

Huguenots, like the work itself, to develop from an elaborately dressed historical pageant into genuine drama. When it does this, however, it makes no mistake about it. Meyerbeer's music rouses itself from its usual short-breathed effectiveness to reach rare heights of passion in Act 4; and the conducting of Richard Bonynge and the dueting of Marilyn Zschau and Anson Austin, cohere in this act of one of the great lyric-dramatic episodes of the Company's history.'

While the run of the *Huguenots* was in progress I had the pleasure of conducting two performances of *Rigoletto* with Yvonne Kenny as Gilda. (This lovely soprano is now doubly well-known throughout the country as the voice of Melba in the very successful eight-hour television drama.) Robert Allman was Rigoletto, Henri Wilden the Duke (replacing the indisposed Luis Lima), Lesley Stender — Maddalena, Erik Badcock — Monterone and Donald Shanks — Sparafucile.

Our last new production for the season was Piccinni's *La Buona Figliuola*, one of the most popular comedies of the eighteenth century but utterly unknown in Australia. This was heavily pre-judged in the Press as obviously being inferior to Mozart and therefore not worth doing. It escaped notice that the work is much superior to a great deal of the lesser Mozart operatic repertoire and in performance the little charmer won many hearts, but not Maria Prerauer's in *The Australian*:

'It is less an opera than an early (1760) ancestor of those empty musical comedies by Lortzing now blessedly exposed to public view only on German-speaking stages. Musically, the hurdy-gurdy score has about as much inspiration as a barrel-organ.'

But Nadine Amadio in *The Sunday Telegraph* thought

'The Australian Opera's new production of Niccolo Piccinni's once popular opera *La Buona Figliuola* (The Good Girl) is indeed an elegant production. It is also witty, charming and highly professional on all levels. It is everything you hope an 18th century music

Right: *Les Huguenots* Act 3 Joan
Sutherland as The Queen; Clifford
Grant as Marcel; Anne-Maree
McDonald as the Page Urbain

theatre entertainment might be. The music, an enchanting blend of Mozart and Gluck,
was given a sparkling performance by the (new to the Company) Australian Chamber
Orchestra under the direction of Richard Bonynge ... The Australian Opera has another
success notched up for the year. Don't miss it.'

The piece which has eight, fairly equal roles was double-cast with Lynne
Cantlon/Anne-Maree McDonald as Cecchina, Constantine Mavridis/Garrick
Jones as Mengotto, Richard Greager/Paul Ferris as the Marquis, Kathleen
Moore/Judith Saliba as Sandrina, Thomas Edmonds/Grahame McFarlane as
Armidoro, Cynthia Johnston/Jennifer Bermingham as Paoluccia, Heather
Begg/Rosemary Gunn as the Marchesa Lucinda and Ronald Maconaghie/Robert
Eddie as Tagliaferro. Because of the use of the Australian Chamber Orchestra the
opera was able to tour during the regular season and twenty performances were
given. After preparing the piece, I was only able to conduct the first three in Sydney.
David Kram took over and conducted the performances in Melbourne, Canberra
and Newcastle, the latter city very rarely visited by The Australian Opera.

As George Kennedy wrote in *The Sydney Sun:*

> 'Marked success crowned The Australian Opera's brave adventure of staging the long-
> forgotten eighteenth century opera buffa of *La Buona Figliuola.'*

Said John Sinclair in *The Melbourne Herald:*

> 'It is not a great or even a very important opera. But it is worth this revival and it is much
> more acceptable than I feared it might be.'

Roger Covell:

> 'There is nothing peripheral about the work or its composer, Niccolo Piccinni (one of the
> most prolific, worthwhile and important composers of 18th century opera), and there-

fore nothing whimsical in principle in wishing to revive it.'

Grahame Bond in *The National Times*:

'Piccinni's style is lighter and more fragile than Mozart's, evoking the ethos of Fragonard and Boucher, of Sèvres and Meissen ... *La Buona Figliuola* is a sentimental *Cinderella* comedy with delightful pre-Mozartian classical style music.'

W.L. Hoffmann wrote in *The Canberra Times*:

'I was surprised at just how good most of it is ... for melodic invention it stands with most other 18th century scores — even in parts with Mozart. I found it a light, attractive, enjoyable production, done with style and humour, and providing a very pleasant evening in the theatre ... some people seem to feel that unless one suffers a little at a performance it cannot really be good, and something that is light and frivolous must therefore be deplored ... I feel sorry for those whose musical noses are held so high, that they cannot enjoy an opera "just for fun".'

Norman Ayrton directed the opera and the ravishing sets and costumes were by Luciana Arrighi.

I must not let the year go by without mentioning the updated adaptation of an amusing Offenbach piece *L'Apotecaire et le Perruquier* which The Australian Opera presented as *Jet-lagged and Jilted* for 108 performances in schools, universities and community centres, even at Taronga Park Zoo. Some 12,000 students were reached in this very worthwhile experiment.

A sad note in the year was the death of Neil Warren-Smith, who had sung firstly with The Elizabethan Trust and then with The Australian Opera for twenty-five years. His deliciously ripe comic performances as Leporello, Dr Bartolo, and Giacomo in *Fra Diavolo*, all of which I performed with him, his Bottom in *A Midsummer Night's Dream*, and his Baron Ochs, both of which I saw, remain wonderful memories of a major artist.

Above Top: La Buona Figliuola (from left to right) Thomas Edmonds as Armidoro, Heather Begg as the Marchioness, Ronald Maconaghie as Tagliaferro, Richard Greager as the Marquis, Lynne Cantlon as Cecchina, Kathleen Moore as Sandrina, and Cynthia Johnston as Paoluccia
Above: La Buona Figliuola Anne-Maree McDonald as Cecchina and Robert Eddie as Tagliaferro

9

NINETEEN EIGHTY TWO

This year was the first year of 'Opera in The Park'. The Australian Opera combined with the Festival of Sydney and its go-ahead Director, Stephen Hall to present *La Traviata* in the Sydney Domain, free to the people. January weather in Sydney is generally very hot but the rain is no respecter of opera managements. The first date — the 16th — was rained out, and the alternative on the following Monday was threatening. But apart from a downpour between Acts 2 and 3 nothing happened to stop the show. The ladies' gowns were muddied and the musicians were very worried about their instruments as there was barely any cover that first year.

Facing Page: Die Fledermaus Act 1. Joan Sutherland as Rosalinde

Lauri Strachan wrote in *The Australian:*

'The lady standing on the grass next to me shouted: "God bless her", and for once, heathen that I am, I was inclined to agree with her. If ever there was a holy communion between a great star and the people who regard her as their own, this was it. Under the rain-torn skies of Sydney's most public of parks, Dame Joan Sutherland sang for her city. And how she sang! There will not be one of the 15,000 or more who ignored the ever-threatening weather to sit on the damp grass of The Domain who will not treasure the memory. This was more than a musical performance, it was a celebration, the stuff of which festivals are made.'

Our season began with that most dangerous of theatrical enterprises — the Triple Bill. Two of the operas were new productions, which I conducted, and the third, Walton's *The Bear*, was a revival, led by David Kram. We opened with William Shield's *Rosina*, an eighteenth century ballad opera which held the stage for nearly fifty years in London since its first performance in 1782 at Covent Garden.

Anne-Maree McDonald sang Rosina, a foundling; Angela Denning — Phoebe; Jennifer Bermingham — William; Rosina Raisbeck — Dorcas; Graham Macfarlane was Mr Belville, Rosina's aristocratic suitor; Paul Ferris, his dissolute brother Captain Belville; Anthony Warlow — a rustic, and Graeme Ewer and Robert Eddie a pair of Irishmen.

In the second piece, *Ba-ta-clan,* Anthony Warlow played Offenbach with Jennifer McGregor as Fé-an-nich-ton and Paul Ferris as Ké-ki-ka-ko, a couple of French nationals shipwrecked on a Chinese island masquerading as Chinese.

Right Top: Rosina (from left to right) Rosina Raisbeck as Dorcas, Jennifer Bermingham as William, Angela Denning as Phoebe and Grahame McFarlane as Belville
Right Below: Rosina (from left to right) Paul Ferris as Captain Belville, Jennifer Bermingham as William and John McKenna as an Irishman

Michael Lewis played the conspirational Ko-ko-ri-ko and Graeme Ewer the reluctant Emperor, Fé-ni-han.

'A very odd, interesting, diverting, gallimaufry of pieces and styles,' wrote Roger Covell in *The Sydney Morning Herald*:

> 'Richard Bonynge's enthusiasm is to be thanked for the first two pieces,which he conducts. They give the Company and its audiences a chance (a welcome one in my view) to widen their notion of what should be done by an opera company in the Opera House.'

Speaking of *Ba-ta-clan*, he said:

Left: Anne-Maree McDonald as Rosina

'The essence of this performance comes in the conjunction of deliberately outrageous settings and costumes and Offenbach's melodious and wonderfully sprightly music with a zany inventiveness of gesture and business that takes wing into the realm of pure, delight-ful nonsense. Michael Lewis, a new member of the Company making an excellent first impression, the soprano Jennifer McGregor, Graeme Ewer (showing a truly genial touch in comedy on this occasion) and Paul Ferris, clinching a splendid comic double with his falsetto tootlings, work with conductor, orchestra, producer, designer and chorus in a mood of mad irresistible fun.'

Nadine Amadio in *The Sunday Telegraph* thought the evening

Above Top: Ba-ta-clan Michael Lewis as Ko-ko-ri-ko, Jennifer McGregor as Fé-an-nich-ton, Graeme Ewer as the Emperor, Paul Ferris as Ké-ki-ka-ko and Anthony Warlow as Offenbach
Above: Graeme Ewer and Michael Lewis as the Emperor Fé-ni-han and Ko-ko-ri-ko in *Ba-ta-clan*

'a great night's entertainment ... the pastoral *Rosina* is an enchanting and melodic work that bridges the gap somewhere between British folk songs and the operas of Haydn'

She also described *Ba-ta-clan* as 'a witty, musical romp'.

The Sun Herald, meanwhile considered it

'the funniest, most original, colourfully made piece of nonsense ever, and a brilliant choice. All Sydney would find it the best entertainment at any theatre. It is a fantastical chinoiserie, and if that is meaningless — go see for yourself.'

Kenneth Rowell designed the amusing set and costumes and Christopher Renshaw directed with witty understanding of the style. We played ten performances in January/February.

Of course, some were not so pleased. Maria Prerauer called it 'puerile slip-on-a-banana-skin musical nonsense' in *The Australian*, and Tony Gould in *The Sun News Pictorial* said

'What possible reason is there for wasting talent, time, and money — much of it taxpayer's money — on this English and French muck?'

A constant diet of roast beef can only become boring. We also need our *hors d'oeuvres* and our desserts. Just for the record, the repertoire for the year consisted of

Salome, Boris Godunov, Falstaff, Macbeth, La Traviata, The Magic Flute, The Bartered Bride, Madama Butterfly, La Bohème, Il Trittico, Lucrezia Borgia, Norma, Cavalleria Rusticana and *Pagliacci, Hamlet, Die Fledermaus, The Rise and Fall of the City of Mahagonny, Patience* and *Manon.* Including the Triple Bill, this added up to twenty-two fairly varied works spread through 216 performances.

During February and the first days of March we revived *Lucrezia Borgia,* in a new set rebuilt for the Concert Hall, for eight performances with some cast changes. Lamberto Furlan sang Gennaro, Bruce Martin and Robert Allman sang Alfonso, and Bernadette Cullen was a handsome Orsini. The Concert Hall, which holds nearly 3,000, has much more opulent acoustics than the smaller Opera Theatre and the performances were deemed even more exciting than the first time round. Of course, there were the odd Donizetti haters, like John Carmody of *The National Times:*

> 'Donizetti writes like a student who has just discovered the diminished seventh chord. What other justification — other than the glorification of Joan Sutherland — can The Australian Opera possibly have for doing such an inferior, unimportant piece?'

Above: Ba-ta-clan The Emperor, Fé-ni-han (Graeme Ewer) sitting on his great cushion

Above Top: Lucrezia Borgia Prologue
(Foreground left) John Wegner as
Gazella and Bernadette Cullen as Orsini
Above: Lucrezia Borgia Act 1. Joan
Sutherland (Lucrezia) and Lamberto
Furlan (Gennaro)

Roger Covell wrote in *The Sydney Morning Herald*

'*Lucrezia Borgia* is one of the most superbly effective operas in which Joan Sutherland
now appears ... it gives everyone who has ever meant to hear this great soprano an opportunity to do so in passionate and varied music that comprehensively shows off her special
gifts ... She and Bonynge, incidentally, have helped to dismiss for ever the notion that
Lucrezia's final aria (whatever the composer had to say about it) is dramatically inappro-
priate. In this performance the sense of high tragedy and passion in the closing solo com-
municates itself strongly and the whole scene becomes an operatic image of brilliant
power ... She could keep this role in her repertoire for another ten years.'

This was a canny prophecy, as Joan sang it in Paris and Barcelona over seven years
later.
W.L. Hoffmann wrote:

'... throughout the performance there was the glory of Sutherland's voice; she seems even
better now than when she sang the role nearly five years ago, as if time is improving her
voice, rather than in any way diminishing its power and beauty.'

At the end of the summer season I revived *Norma* for four performances with Rita
Hunter, who is one of the very few sopranos today with the amplitude, quality and
agility of voice to encompass the role. Anson Austin and Rosemary Gunn sang
Pollione and Adalgisa, and Clifford Grant was his usual sonorous Oroveso.

After Sydney we went to Perth, which is such a lovely city, for a recital which was televised and later sold as a videotape. I returned to Sydney at the end of May to begin rehearsals for Ambroise Thomas' *Hamlet* which was to receive its Australian première on 9 June. Sherrill Milnes came from the Metropolitan Opera, New York, to sing the title role and Joan Carden was to have sung Ophélie. An unfortunate car accident removed Joan Carden from the cast and gave Jennifer McGregor the opportunity to endear herself to the public with her finest singing in a role for which she was temperamentally and physically suited. Heather Begg turned in yet another strong performance as the Queen, with Bruce Martin as her husband, Claudius. Richard Greager was Laerte, Robin Donald — Marcellus, John Fulford — Horatio, Clifford Grant — The Ghost, John Wegner — Polonius and the Grave-diggers were Gordon Wilcock and John Germain. The handsome production was by Lotfi Mansouri with sets by Allan Lees, costumes by Desmond Digby and choreography by Robert Ray. The opera was sung in the original French and performed eight times in Sydney during June and July.

It was pre-judged a disaster by many of the Press but W.L. Hoffmann of *The Canberra Times* had the grace to contradict himself:

Above: Lucrezia Borgia Act 2. with Bruce Martin as Alfonso

Above: Norma Act 1. Rosemary Gunn
(Adalgisa) and Anson Austin
(Pollione)
Right: Norma Act 4. Rita Hunter
(Norma) and Clifford Grant (Oroveso)

'In writing my previous comments I had to rely on what I thought were authoritative sources: this caused me to make the statement that "the only resemblance between Shakespeare's play and the libretto is in the names of the characters and some of the more dramatic moments". When I saw The Australian Opera production last Saturday, I realised how ridiculously wrong that statement was — obviously the writers I had quoted from had never seen the opera produced either! For the libretto is quite a skilful condensation of Shakespeare's play which works well as an opera, retaining the essential dramatic elements of the play, and certainly the equal of the libretto for Verdi's *Macbeth*. And Thomas's music not only has a strong melodic line but has a dramatic impact at appropriate moments which I found quite surprising, considering the deprecating comments it receives from most histories of opera.'

But Maria Prerauer in *The Australian* called it

'at times enjoyably awful … the awfulness comes from the music; trite, ignoble, predictable and soap operettish. And from the libretto's fascinatingly horrible travesty of Shakespeare.'

Roger Covell in *The Sydney Morning Herald:*

'The truth as revealed by The Australian Opera's fine and persuasive performance of the work, needs to be stated quite simply. Thomas's *Hamlet* is an effective, continuously absorbing opera, often memorable and sometimes moving … Thomas's major achievement in *Hamlet* is his response to the big challenges of the drama. The encounter between Hamlet and his mother and uncle, the scene on the battlements (almost universally praised), the mimed play (with Hamlet as Chorus) are sensitively and strongly expressed in a musical-dramatic language that is direct, appropriate and vivid … That leaves one circumstance with the capacity to shock an English-speaking audience. When I noted the extent of the Act 4 ballet sequence (obligatory in Parisian opera of its period), I assumed that The Australian Opera would cut all or most of it. Bonynge as musical director and Lotfi Mansouri as producer, have decided, instead, to retain it. The more I think about it the more I am convinced they are right. For one thing, it emphasises the fact that the operatic *Hamlet* is a work in its own right, not to be judged only by

Left: Hamlet Act 2. Jennifer McGregor
(Ophélie) and Sherrill Milnes (Hamlet)

Above: Hamlet Act 4. The Ballet
Right: Hamlet Act 1. Heather Begg as
Gertrude and Bruce Martin as Claudius

Shakespearean canons; belonging to an independent tradition. For another, what seems at first only a eupeptic essay in peasant merrymaking in the manner of *Giselle*, Act 1, becomes a surprisingly touching background for the entrance of mad Ophelia, picturesquely fey with flowers in her hair … Thomas's *Hamlet* is worth reviving and well worth attending.'

The cast was a very strong one and I confess to having had enormous pleasure

from this great old warhorse.

For light relief we had a new production of Johann Strauss' *Die Fledermaus* which opened on 25 June for twelve performances. The production was by Anthony Besch and the design by John Stoddart.

Eisenstein was played by Robert Gard and Ronald Stevens; Alfred by Anson Austin and Paul Ferris; Adele by Monique Brynnel and Jennifer McGregor; Orlofsky by Heather Begg; Blind by Gordon Wilcock; Falke by Michael Lewis; Frank by Gregory Yurisich; and Frosch by Graeme Ewer. 'The Grand Pas de Deux' from *Don Quixote* was danced in the party scene by Lois Strike and Kelvin Coe.

'Any notion that Dame Joan is slumming in the part of Rosalinde or coasting through an easy evening should be put firmly out of mind,' wrote Roger Covell in *The Sydney Morning Herald:*

'She sings with grace, phenomenal accuracy, humour and affection; and she demon-

Above: Die Fledermaus Act 2. (Left to right) Robert Gard (Eisenstein), Joan Sutherland (Rosalinde) and Heather Begg (Orlovsky)

strates once again her gift for comedy (not high comedy, something closer to fun). Her Zsa Zsa Gabor accent when she has to pretend to be a Hungarian Countess is really very good; as the disguised Rosalinde in Act 2 she skips about the stage with surprising nimbleness ... And she is characteristically ready to take a joke against herself. When Frosch the jailer — Graeme Ewer at his most teetering and spavined, with an amiable baby's smile — informs the house in Act 3 that there is a lady outside — "a very big girl for her size" if I heard him correctly — the audience has no doubt (and is not meant to have any) who will make the next entrance.'

W.L. Hoffmann wrote:

'The chorus singing and orchestral playing had a Viennese lilt, and Bonynge even managed to imbue the well-known overture with a special character which set the mood for the whole performance. I have seen Strauss operetta done in Vienna, but this Australian Opera production could hold its own anywhere, even in Strauss's own city of "wine, women and song".'

The whole cast of tremendously good comedians had great fun and this was the first Australian Opera performance to be telecast live — and issued subsequently on

video cassette. As a result, Joan and the Opera Company between them received some 45,000 letters!

On 17 July we opened a new production of Massenet's *Manon* for ten performances of which I conducted the first eight. Directed by John Copley with designs by Kristian Fredrikson this was the first time the Company had performed *Manon*. Glenys Fowles sang the title role with Richard Greager and Anson Austin as the Chevalier des Grieux. John Pringle and Michael Lewis sang Lescaut; Clifford Grant the Comte des Grieux; Graeme Ewer, Guillot; John Fulford, de Bretigny; and the three euphemistically called 'actresses' were played by Narelle Davidson, Cynthia Johnston and Bernadette Cullen.

'After the gritty muesli of *Mahagonny*, Sydney opera-goers have been returned to the staple junk-food of this winter's diet with the marshmallow of Massenet's *Manon*,' wrote John Carmody in *The National Times*. But thankfully he was in the minority. Maria Prerauer made the comparison with Puccini's *Manon Lescaut*:

> 'At the Sydney Opera House Puccini's did not work. At its first night on Saturday Massenet's did. Yet Puccini, it must be said, is by far the more important composer, even though his *Manon Lescaut* is an early flawed attempt. However, *Manon* is Massenet's mature masterpiece and much better theatre all round. Conductor Richard Bonynge seems to be at his best in this sort of music. He brings out the typical nineteenth-century sentimentality and its cloying eroticism of withered rose-petals most beguilingly.'

Above: Die Fledermaus Act 1. With Robert Gard as von Eisenstein, (left) and Gordon Wilcock as Dr Blind

George Kennedy in *The Sun* called *Manon*

> 'a great achievement ... Jules Massenet's *Manon* is perhaps the zenith of lyric opera and John Copley's production is lavishly rich and Richard Bonynge's musical direction authoritative ... Glenys Fowles Manon is her most accomplished performance in this country. She is versatile and musical — a singing actress who is a pleasure to see and hear ... Conductor Bonynge showed his deep feeling for the nineteenth-century French Opera repertoire. He kept a strong grip on the ensemble to prevent any overplay and allowed the singers to be heard although the orchestra never lost its presence.'

Roger Covell, critic for *The Sydney Morning Herald*, found the evening 'perpetually fascinating' and thought the Company's sense of ensemble outstanding. And from the W.L. Hoffman of *The Canberra Times*:

> '... dramatic tension builds up steadily to a third act which has considerable impact and which gives the lie to the sometimes expressed opinion that Massenet's music is sweet, sentimental and non-dramatic ... Richard Bonynge conducts, and again displays that particular affinity for and understanding of French opera which he has shown before. This is a handsome presentation of this most attractive and melodious opera, excellently sung and authoritively conducted.'

Manon was a happy finale to the Sydney season. If I have any regrets — and I rarely waste any time in that way — it is that *Manon* was the only opera of Massenet which we played during my eleven seasons with The Australian Opera.

The year ended with a surplus of $245,000, a reversal of the 1981 deficit of $834,000.

Above Top: Die Fledermaus Act 2. Monique Brynnel as Adele with Catherine Elliott (left) and Dorothy Robertson-O'Brien
Above: Manon Glenys Fowles as Manon Act 1
Facing Page: Manon (from left to right) Cynthia Johnston as Javotte, Bernadette Cullen as Rosette, Glenys Fowles as Manon and Narelle Davidson as Pousette

10

NINETEEN EIGHTY THREE

The year began with a revival of *Die Fledermaus* — Joan sang two Rosalindes in the theatre and one in the open-air, and Marilyn Richardson sang three in the theatre. The park performance this year was favoured with perfect weather and around one hundred thousand people turned out — the atmosphere was magical. Leonie Rysanek, who was currently singing Tosca with the Company, joined us for the party scene and sang a wonderful 'Meine Lippen Sie küssen so heiss' from Lehár's *Giuditta*.

Luciano Pavarotti fulfilled a promise to us of a few years back to come to Australia, and he sang three *Bohèmes* in Sydney as well as a recital in Melbourne. He joined Joan and myself in a grand operatic gala in the Concert Hall which realised the largest box office ever for an indoor event in Australia — close to $300,000. The ticket prices were extortionate but the event was sold out — it was also simulcast and marketed as a videotape. The excitement was shared, too, by television viewers in New Zealand and radio listeners across the United States. A survey in Melbourne and Sydney indicated that six million viewers watched, making it one of the highest-rating single performances in Australian television history.

Pavarotti carried on a great deal about an allergy to stage dust, which reminded one of Melba's fleas on the train, and like Melba he reaped a great deal of publicity for his efforts.

Gounod's *Roméo et Juliette* was the first new production of the summer season — directed in the Concert Hall by Sir Robert Helpmann and spectacularly designed by Kenneth Rowell. This rather balletic production gave immense pleasure. Glenys Fowles sang Juliet and Anson Austin, Roméo, with John Pringle as Mercutio, Clifford Grant as Friar Lawrence, Anne-Maree MacDonald as Stephano and Heather Begg as Gertrude. Tybalt was sung by Paul Ferris, Paris by Anthony Warlow, Capulet by Donald Shanks and Bruce Martin, Gregorio by John Antoniou, Benvolio by Robin Donald, the Duke of Verona by John Wegner and Friar John by Constantine Mavridis.

W.L. Hoffmann wrote in *The Canberra Times:*

> 'In Australia the particular interest of Richard Bonynge in the 19th century French opera
> has meant that since he has been musical director of The Australian Opera we have been
> able to see productions of some of these little-known works — the *Lakmé* of Delibes,
> Massenet's *Manon*, the *Hamlet* of Thomas, and Meyerbeer's *Les Huguenots*.

Facing Page: Luciano Pavarotti and Joan Sutherland in the Gala Concert

To add to these, The Australian Opera's first production of Gounod's *Roméo et Juliette* is included in the current Sydney Summer Season, being given a large-scale presentation in the Concert Hall.

It is a very impressive production with an ingenious setting designed by Kenneth Rowell which suggests an amphitheatre, in which the action is played, behind which the ancient houses of an Italian town rise up a hillside in serried ranks. It may not be Verona, but it is effectively atmospheric.

Robert Helpmann has given the production stylish direction, and with Bonynge conducting the performances and getting equally stylish playing from the orchestra, Gounod's lyric opera is given every opportunity to make its full impression.

Add to that the fine singing from all the cast, and it is not hard to see why this lovely opera was Gounod's greatest success and had such world-wide popularity a century ago.

Anson Austin as Roméo and Glenys Fowles as Juliette are an attractive and believable pair of "star-crossed lovers" singing throughout with great beauty of tone and line in their solos, and in particular in their four lyrical love duets, which are the musical core of the opera.'

Above: Roméo et Juliette Act 1. Anthony Warlow as Paris and Paul Ferris as Tybalt
Far Left Top: Roméo et Juliette Act 2. John Pringle (Mercutio); Anson Austin (Roméo) and Paul Ferris (Tybalt) with Vincenzo Nesci, Constantine Mavridis and Donald Solomon
Far Left Below: Roméo et Juliette Anne-Maree McDonald as Stephano with (left to right) Louise Napier, Richard Jones, Judith Turner, Lindsay Mika, Theo Connors, John Miley and Ann-Patricia Hemingway.

Above: Roméo et Juliette Last act. Glenys Fowles as Juliette; Anson Austin as Roméo

Frank Harris wrote in *The Daily Mirror:*

'Most credit goes to Richard Bonynge who conducted the Elizabethan Sydney Orchestra and The Australian Opera Chorus with fine appreciation of the delectable score. As the tragic couple … Glenys Fowles and Anson Austin were ideally matched; Glenys was an enchanting and utterly believable young Juliet. Austin projected a bold and handsome Romeo, gathering strength, warmth and passion vocally as the story darkened with sadness.'

Roger Covell paid a second visit to hear

'Bruce Martin's warmly sonorous and commanding voice … rolling round the ample spaces of the concert hall with full firm tone and ample volume. Richard Bonynge's wholly sympathetic direction has deepened in its intuitive response to the score. His support of the soloists is now a model of timing and discretion and is certainly calculated to bring out the best in the major individual performances. I count his conducting of this opera as among the best work he has done here … I find myself further in love with Gounod's lyrically passionate score after revisiting this production.'

We decided to revive the 1981 *Alcina* for seven performances in February with some changes of cast. Joan sang Alcina, the role which she had sung for her Italian

Left: Alcina Act 2

Above: Alcina Act 1 with Margreta Elkins (Ruggiero)

débat in Venice in 1960. She also sang the first British performances of the opera since the 18th century, in 1957. Margreta Elkins again sang Ruggiero, Lauris Elms — Bradamante, Jennifer McGregor — Morgana, Anne-Maree McDonald — Oberto, Richard Greager — Oronte and John Wegner — Melisso.

George Kennedy in *The Sun* wrote that *Alcina*

'has become one of the most important repertory pieces of the Australian Opera, as conceived at its revival last week. The sheer beauty of John Pascoe's dazzling settings and Sir Robert Helpmann's sensitive production perfectly mirrored Handel's music-theatre which was a never-ending struggle for recognition in the hotbed of Opera seria.

The performance was crowned by Dame Joan Sutherland's playing of the name part. The ravishing beauty of her voice, the easiness of how she executed the most difficult passages in Alcina's six arias and how she tormented herself in between love, jealousy, bitterness and despair — kept one sitting at the edge of the seat. The capacity audience

Above: Alcina Act 1

certainly were rewarded by a tremendous account of "Ah, mio cor" in Act 2 when she learns that Ruggiero plans to leave her — one of the greatest that even Sutherland could have given.'

Frank Harris in *The Mirror* thought Joan

'sang with glorious vocal power, ranging from tender love to jealously and finally to destructive rage as her magical powers failed her.'

Maria Prerauer wrote:

'Dame Joan Sutherland in radiant voice took over the title role of the wicked enchantress … if she didn't seem terribly wicked she certainly enchanted.'

Roger Covell spoke of

'feats of legerity and vocal panache of which the average soprano can only dream.'

Pip Rath in *The Bulletin* wrote of

'a veritable orgy of quasi-baroque opulence of an order The Australian Opera is unlikely to be able to afford again … Joan Sutherland's return to this opera, in which she first earned the "La Stupenda" tag in the late '50s, is worth all the scenery Pascoe and Helpmann could throw at their audience. She is simply electrifying as the wicked enchantress Alcina.'

At the end of February there were terrible bushfires in Victoria and South Australia, causing major catastrophies. My conductor colleagues, Geoffrey Arnold, Stuart Challender, Peter Seymour, David Kram, William Reid and Carlo Felice Cillario joined over thirty soloists, the chorus and orchestra in a Benefit Concert on

Above: Lucia di Lammermoor Act 1
Scene 2 Jennifer McGregor

Sunday, 27 February at 1 pm, the day after our last *Alcina* when we were due to leave.
Joan and I were able to appear in the first half and dash off to catch a plane to Europe
that afternoon for our next lot of engagements. The programme was very long —
Joan and Margreta Elkins sang the 'Mira o Norma' scene and the first half ended
with the Sextet from *Lucia di Lammermoor*. I particularly remember accompanying
Ladislav Jasek, our concertmaster, playing the 'Méditation' from *Thaïs* most beautifully.

Our first performance on returning for the Winter Season was a gala to raise
money for the Australian Auditions Committee. This organisation, energetically

Above: Il Trovatore Jonathan Summers as Di Luna
Left: Il Trovatore Act 4 Joan Sutherland as Leonora

led by Mrs Sheila Prior, did much for opera, and presented each year a Joan Sutherland Scholarship of ten thousand dollars to a deserving young singer.

Joan sang arias by Mozart, Bellini and Shield, and John Noble gave the first modern performance of a Rossini bassoon concerto written when he was sixteen years of age, which I had discovered in a Vancouver Library. James Kortum played a Boccherini flute concerto and the Johann Christian Bach, *C Major Sinfonia Concertante* was played by James Kortum, Graham Powning, Ladislav Jasek and Nigel Parry.

After Jennifer McGregor's great success in *Hamlet*, it was decided to revive *Lucia di Lammermoor* for her. This was a psychologically daunting project for her, being well aware that she was following Joan in her most famous role. But Jenny has strong inner resources and brought her youth and charm to the role. *The Sun's* opera critic thought

'she painted a touching, lyrical and fragile portrait of Lucia.'

She was joined in these performance by Anson Austin, John Fulford and Graeme Ewer singing Edgardo, Enrico and Arturo for the first time. Rosina Raisbeck and Clifford Grant gave solid support to the debutantes and the nine performances were very enjoyable from my point of view.

Between 15 June and 22 July there was a new production of *Il Trovatore* with décor

Right: Il Trovatore Act 2 Lauris Elms as Azucena and Kenneth Collins, Manrico

by Sidney Nolan and costumes by Luciana Arrighi. It was considered a coup to have the great Australian painter design an opera — he had previously designed Saint-Saëns' *Samson* for Covent Garden — and the artist most generously donated his original paintings for the drops to The Australian Opera.

Disaster almost overtook us near the first night when Francisco Ortiz, the Spanish tenor, fell ill. Australia, in common with most countries, is not full of dramatic tenors, especially ones with high C's, and since the retirement of Donald Smith we were in trouble. Fortunately the Welsh tenor, Kenneth Collins, was free to fly out and save the day. Fortunately also, for The Australian Opera he liked Australia and took up residence, which certainly alleviated casting problems. 'His high C at the end of "Di quella pira" is triumphant in its sustained ring and firmness' wrote Roger Covell in *The Sydney Morning Herald,* and he also thought that Lauris Elms as Azucena 'gave one of the great performances of her career'.

It was a pleasure to work again (and twice in the one year) with Lauris, whom we had known since the fifties when she and Joan sang together at Covent Garden in Handel's *Samson.*

'Joan Sutherland as Leonora lets us hear how superbly equipped she is to under-

Above: The Barber of Seville Elizabeth Fretwell as Berta
Left Top: The Barber of Seville Clifford Grant as Basilio and Gregory Yurisich as Bartolo
Left Below: The Barber of Seville Trio in Act 2. Hakan Hagegard, Jennifer McGregor and Thomas Edmonds (Figaro, Rosina and Almaviva)

take a role of heroic proportions,' wrote Covell, and in her final aria he praised a 'final trill of a length and finish such as no other singer of recent times could rival'.

Nadine Amadio in *The Sunday Telegraph* wrote

'The magnificent music of Verdi's *Il Trovatore* was brought to electrifying life ... Dame Joan Sutherland's handling of the demanding role of Leonora was an example of professional opera stagecraft and stunning vocal beauty ... when one added to this great singing the powerful imagery of Sidney Nolan, the surprisingly calm authority of Richard Bonynge and the strong chessboard direction of Elijah Moshinsky, it resulted in a memorable night at the opera.'

Above: Semiramide Act 4
Right: Semiramide Bruce Martin as Assur

The Catholic Weekly wrote

'From the start Joan Sutherland is never less than magnificent, her Leonora one of heroic proportions, singing with that superlative power of hers with admirable purity, her voice seemingly better than ever with its truly thrilling trills ... The opera boasts not only a fine chorus, but a spirited orchestra from which Richard Bonynge obtained some of the best playing he has ever got, tight, delicate and inspired in turns.'

The Australian baritone, Jonathan Summers, who had been singing in Covent Garden, sang his first performances as di Luna and phrased aristocratically. Donald Shanks was Ferrando, Cynthia Johnston — Inez, John Durham — a gypsy and Robin Donald — Ruiz. The production was televised live and issued as a video cassette.

During August, *The Barber of Seville* was revived for ten performances, of which I conducted the first six. I say a revival but it was reproduced by Christopher Renshaw with the existing designs of Roger Butlin. Jennifer McGregor sang Rosina; Thomas Edmonds — Almaviva, Hakan Hagegard — Figaro, Gregory Yurisich — Dr Bartolo,

Clifford Grant — Basilio and Elizabeth Fretwell — Berta with John Antoniou as Fiorello, Donald Solomon as Ambrogio and Joseph Grunfelder, the Officer.

Nadine Amadio wrote in *The Sunday Telegraph:*

> 'The Australian Opera's new season of Rossini's *Il Barbiere di Siviglia* is lively, entertaining and bubbling with good-humoured musical fun. Rossini's witty and enchanting music hasn't faded with the years and is well presented by this team of enthusiastic and talented vocalists and musicians. The young Swedish baritone, Hakan Hagegard, making his first appearance with The Australian Opera, is a professional and attractive Figaro, with a firm rich voice he blends graciously with the Company. Conductor Richard Bonynge, a master of Rossini's style, draws a caring and enjoyable performance from the Elizabethan Sydney Orchestra. Jennifer McGregor is in sparkling voice and looks charming as Rosina. It's a role that suits her admirably and she makes the most of it. One of the bonuses of the new season is Gregory Yurisich as Doctor Bartolo. He is an outstanding vocalist and has quite a gift for comedy. Thomas Edmonds, in excellent voice, plays the comic side of his role well … a fine performance from Clifford Grant and a good supporting cast make this *Barber* a winner.'

Of the supporting cast I have the nicest memories of Don Solomon's very funny yawning Ambrogio and Elizabeth Fretwell's superb Berta. I remember coaching her in the roles of Violetta and Leonora in the very early fifties in London and for years since leaving Sadler's Wells she has sung so many of the great soprano roles with The Australian Opera.

In the lesson scene, Jenny McGregor sang the very difficult Proch Variations so beloved of the great prime donne of yesterday.

Also during August we gave five performances of Rossini's *Semiramide.* It had originally been intended to give the opera in a semi-staged version — little more than a concert version. But in the event a 'mise-en-scène' was evolved by Rodney Clark from scenic elements in stock using mostly stock costumes. As we were constantly rebuked for spending so much money we thought this gesture would be well received. Not at all — just huge complaints about the lack of grandeur and spectacle. Our production certainly did not resemble that of La Scala but it was most adequate and good to look at, and directed with the minimum of fuss by Moffatt Oxenbould. And, of course, it served the purpose of letting the public see and hear an opera not

Right: Die Fledermaus (from left to right) Anne-Maree McDonald and Jennifer McGregor as Ida and Adele

seen in the country for nearly twenty years.

Lauris Elms sang Arsace, as she had with Joan in 1965, Anson Austin, Idreno and Bruce Martin, Assur with Anne-Maree McDonald as Azema, Clifford Grant as the Ghost of Nino, Constantine Mavridis as Oroe and Anthony Warlow as Mitrane.

The Company has no business to be presenting such mush,' said Mrs Prerauer, although she acknowledged 'glorious, highly-embroidered singing.'

Brian Hoad in *The Bulletin*:

> 'It's splendid music ... and it's splendidly sung ... at its centre sails Joan Sutherland tossing off appropriately insane floods of vocal trills and roulades and curlicues and whirligigs as the demented Queen of Babylon ... certainly Sutherland's extraordinary performance receives strong support from her associates who are also called on to tackle coloratura demands beyond the normal call of duty.'

W.L. Hoffmann in *The Canberra Times* wrote:

> 'The opening night of The Australian Opera's first presentation of Rossini's *bel-canto* opera *Semiramide* ... provided a feast of magnificent singing. With Sutherland in the title role of the Queen of Babylonia there was the promise of memorable vocalism, and the promise was certainly fulfilled. It was in 1962 that she revived the role for La Scala, and, listening to the glorious outpouring of assured tonal splendour she produced on Friday night, one could not imagine that she could have sung it any better on that occasion twenty years ago ... Richard Bonynge conducted and the orchestral playing maintained the excellent standard that the Elizabethan Sydney Orchestra is now achieving, bringing out the subtle touches of Rossini's scoring in this opera.'

Left: Die Fledermaus Act 1 Finale. With Gregory Yurisich as Frank and Ronald Stevens as Eisenstein

Having had experience of the opera with many and varied singers, I am happy to report that our cast stood beside the best. Lauris Elms' rich-toned Arsace, Anson Austin's brilliant stratospheric Idreno and Bruce Martin's black-voiced menacing Assur deserve the highest praise.

On 19 August, I had the pleasure of launching the autobiography of Lindley Evans, *Hello, Mr Melody Man*, at the Sydney Conservatorium. The last accompanist of Melba, and my piano teacher to whom I owe so much, he did an immense amount to popularise music in Australia, especially in his work with young people.

The entire year had encompassed nineteen operas — 198 performances in all. Besides those new productions already mentioned there was a new *Così fan tutte* and a new *Walküre*. A tour to the country towns of Armidale, Grafton, Lismore, Newcastle and Tamworth was organised with several of our young artists.

There was a $607,000 surplus of income over expenditure, and the box office realised $7,180,000, compared with $5,823,000 in the previous year.

11

NINETEEN EIGHTY FOUR

1984 began with eight performances of *The Magic Flute* — with Yvonne Kenny an enchanting Pamina, Richard Greager — Tamino, Anthony Warlow — Papageno, Christa Leahmann — the Queen of the Night, Donald Shanks — Sarastro, John Pringle — the Speaker, Christopher Dawes — Monostatos and Cynthia Johnston — Papagena.

Facing Page: The Dialogues of the Carmelites as Madame Lidoine

George Kennedy wrote in *The Sydney Sun*:

'The Australian Opera's ten-year-old production of Mozart's *Magic Flute* has never sounded and looked brighter, or been stronger on pathos and magic than in its latest revival under the musical direction of Richard Bonynge.'

Both debutantes were highly praised. As the Queen, Christa Leahmann

'here makes an impressive début in a proper star-blazing fury,'

said *The Bulletin*, and

The highly promising début Papageno of Anthony Warlow was the clear highlight of John Copley's eleven-year-old *Magic Flute*,'

wrote David Gyger in *Opera Australia.*

Shortly after the opening of *The Magic Flute* we had the yearly opera in the park. A new mobile sound shell was used so that the performers were less at the mercy of the elements than previously but the public were still vulnerable. This performance of *Lucia* marked the twenty-fifth anniversary of Joan's first Covent Garden performance in the role in 1959, almost to the day. Her Edgardo was Richard Greager, Enrico — John Fulford, and Raimondo — Clifford Grant.

Roger Covell wrote in *The Sydney Morning Herald*:

'With a white shawl around her shoulders as her only concession to the damp breeziness of Sydney's night air, she sang with as much fervour and mastery for her non-paying audience as if they had been occupying the most expensive seats in the Opera House, the Met, Covent Garden or La Scala.'

Above: The Magic Flute Act 2. Anthony
Warlow and Cynthia Johnston as
Papageno and Papagena
Right: The Magic Flute Act 1.
(Left to right) John Pringle (The
Speaker); Yvonne Kenny (Pamina);
Neville Grave (1st Priest) and Donald
Shanks (Sarastro)
Facing Page: Adriana Lecouvreur Act 1

Over one hundred thousand turned out for the event including the Prime
Minister, the Premier and the Lord Mayor, and down came the rain, no respecter of
persons, just as the performance ended.

The first new production of the year was Cilea's *Adriana Lecouvreur* in a *fin-de-
siècle* production in the manner of Sarah Bernhardt, herself a famous Adrienne in
the original play by Scribe and Legouvé. John Copley directed and the beautiful sets
and costumes were by Alan Lees and Michael Stennett. We gave ten performances
during January and February.

The strong cast included Anson Austin as Maurizio, Heather Begg as the
Princess, John Shaw as Michonnet, John Wegner as the Prince and Graeme Ewer as
the Abbé. The actresses Jouvenot and Dangeville were played by Judith Saliba and
Jennifer Bermingham and the actors, Poisson and Quinault, by Christopher Dawes
and Robert Eddie. Young Jeffrey Black, of whom much has been heard since, made
his début as the Major-domo, but in the television performance sang Quinault, due
to the indisposition of Robert Eddie, with great aplomb.

The usual muck was written, or shall I say repeated, about *Adriana* being merely a
star vehicle with one tune but many critics and the public received it as the master-
work it is.

There was a great deal of controversy due to the introduction for the first time in
Australia of surtitles. They undoubtedly help a large part of the audience to understand the ramifications of the plot and I do not understand those who are so strongly
against them. As they are above the proscenium arch, one only sees them if one
makes the effort.

Above Top: Adriana Lecouvreur Act 3
Heather Begg as the Princess and
Graeme Ewer as the Abbé
Above: Adriana Lecouvreur Act 4 with
John Shaw as Michonnet, (left) and
Anson Austin as Maurizio
Right: Adriana Lecouvreur Act 3

Peter Robinson in *Australian Financial Review*:

'*Adriana* is a gross waste of a national treasure ... ludicrous, banal, extravagant.'

Maria Prerauer in *Opera*:

'Richard Bonynge's musical direction brought out all the highly-coloured B-Grade Hollywood soundtrack effects which are built into the trashy score.'

W.L. Hoffmann in *The Canberra Times*:

'This is an excellently sung, played and staged production of this lovely, lyrical opera; that it has taken eighty years to achieve a performance in Australia is quite surprising. It makes a welcome addition to the repertoire and is a change from the seemingly endless repetition of the round dozen of popular Puccini and Verdi operas we have been getting in recent years.'

The Daily Mirror thought that

'Dame Joan Sutherland enchanted a sell-out audience as the star of a new production of Cilea's romantic drama *Adriana Lecouvreur* ... Dame Joan richly dressed in Michael Stennett's gorgeous costumes not only looked and acted like a theatre star but sang magnificently.'

Above: The Merry Widow Gordon Wilcock as Baron Zeta, Graeme Ewer as Njegus, and Robert Gard as Danilo
Above Left: The Merry Widow Jennifer Bermingham as Zozo and Robert Eddie as Cascada
Left: Trial by Jury Anthony Warlow as the Defendant and Anne-Maree McDonald as the Plaintiff with the Bridesmaids

David Gyger thought she fulfilled splendidly the dramatic requirements in

'perhaps the most fully realised operatic performance, all round, I have yet to experience from her … she fully justified The Australian Opera's decision to mount *Adriana*.'

The Melbourne Sun:

'If I have left the important orchestral contribution for the last, it is because I wish to pay a special tribute to Richard Bonynge and his players for the refinement and sensitiveness

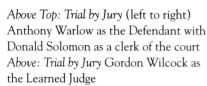

Above Top: Trial by Jury (left to right)
Anthony Warlow as the Defendant with
Donald Solomon as a clerk of the court
Above: Trial by Jury Gordon Wilcock as
the Learned Judge
Right: Trial by Jury (left to right) John
Germain as the Usher, John Fulford as
the Counsel for the Plaintiff, and Anne-
Maree McDonald as the Plaintiff

of musical treatment, when the conductor nursed his singers with such care, that the music folds itself around them like a beautiful garment, rather than in other hands and at other times, like a drowning wave.'

The result is there for all to see on the videotape which was released following the simulcast.

On 11 February the Australian Broadcasting Commission presented a feature, 'Sutherland, a Celebration' to celebrate the tenth year of Joan's association with The Australian Opera. She was seen rehearsing for *Adriana*, talking about her roles, and introducing excerpts from *Lucia, The Widow, Don Giovanni, La Traviata* and *Die Fledermaus*.

Beginning 15 February, *The Merry Widow* again made her re-appearance with the delicious Swedish-Australian soprano, Monique Brynnel, who, according to Maria Prerauer, 'oozed sexy charm, looked pretty and sang with panache.'

In this revival Robert Gard sang Danilo, Rosamund Illing — Valencienne, Thomas Edmonds — Camille and Jennifer Bermingham — Zozo. With Gordon Wilcock and Graeme Ewer in their usual roles we had lots of laughs.

Roger Covell in *The Sydney Morning Herald:*

'In conducting it with a spirit and dedication at least as considerable as he brings to the serious moments of opera, Bonynge is the person who deserves most of the credit for answering the question of how to present *The Merry Widow* in the Concert Hall and how to animate the occasion with lilting appeal and driving energy. His presentation of Lehar's score is of quite extraordinary merit.'

On 26 February, the Elizabethan Sydney Orchestra inaugurated a series of Sunday Serenades. I conducted the first of these, the programme including the *Petite*

Above: Ba-ta-clan Jennifer McGregor (Fé-an-nich-ton), Graeme Ewer as Fé-ni-han, and Paul Ferris as Ké-ki-ka-ko
Left: Ba-ta-clan Paul Ferris as Ké-ki-ka-ko and Jennifer McGregor as Fé-an-nich-ton

Above: Costume design for *Ba-ta-clan* by
Kenneth Rowell
Right: Ba-ta-clan The chorus

Symphonie of Gounod, the Ibert *Divertissement* and the *Bachianas brasileiras No 5* of Villa-Lobos with Jennifer McGregor as the brilliant soloist. The concert was held in the Great Hall of the Conservatorium where I had been a student in the forties when Eugene Goossens was the Director. Although I rarely enjoy conducting concerts, the conjunction of a nostalgic visit to my old haunts and working with people I knew and liked made this an exception.

On returning to Sydney after nearly four months abroad, I was met with the news that Mr Veitch and the Board had decided that the Opera Company did not need a Music Director and that they had changed Moffatt's title from Artistic Administrator to Artistic Director. This was certainly a power move on Veitch's part

Above Top: Les Contes d'Hoffmann Act
1. Bernadette Cullen as Nicklausse
Above: Les Contes d'Hoffmann as
Giulietta
Right: Les Contes d'Hoffmann as Antonia
Facing Page: Les Contes d'Hoffmann
Graeme Ewer as, (clockwise from top
left) Andrès, Cochenille, Frantz and
Pitichinaccio

which, in fact, did him no good. I think the Music Board of Australia Council may
have had something to do with it — I was diametrically opposed to wasting money
on unproven Australian operas and believed that they should be first given in exper-
imental circumstances. Also I never played the political game beloved by all those
on the fringe of the arts in Australia — it just bored me.

I am not quite sure what purpose was served. Moffatt and I had always made decisions in tandem and life went on as usual. For me in most ways it was a welcome
relief. I have always hated responsibility — I loathed refusing requests from singers
(many of whom were my friends) for roles — and I detested sacking people. Anyone
who had glanced through this book will realise that with the number of performances I conducted and with the inherent rehearsals, I had little time for administration. I had always left this in Moffatt's hands — he had always done half my work
and half the General Manager's as well. He was a real workaholic! So business just
went on as usual for the next three years. The Company continued to pay my salary
as Musical Director to the end of 1986, my title remained in all programmes until the
end of that year, and I did my best to earn the money — as I always had.

Although Mr Veitch and the Board behaved in an ungentlemanly manner, they
did me a favour — it was the same decision I would have had to make sooner or later.
My tastes in music are my own but they correspond exactly to what, before my time
with the Company, was missing from The Australian Opera repertory. There was little understanding of *bel canto*, there was almost no French repertoire and no explo-
ration of the eighteenth-century. I believe I opened these doors and that Joan and I
left a legacy which is continuing and will continue. I don't believe the time and
energy were wasted. I now look back on my eleven years with the Company as
Musical Director with great satisfaction and very happy memories. I dare say some of
my decisions were better than others but I regret none of them.

And so on with the season. Beginning on 14 July we played a new version of the
Triple Bill, for eight performances, called *An Evening with Gilbert, Offenbach and*

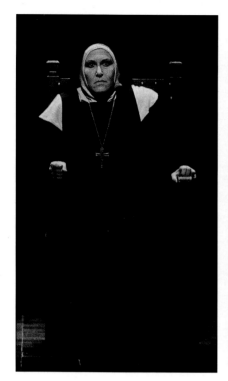

Above: The Dialogues of the Carmelites
Lone Koppel as the old Prioress
Right: Isobel Buchanan as Blanche in
The Dialogues of the Carmelites

Sullivan. This time *Ba-ta-clan* was played last, as anything after it must needs be anti-climactic. We began with Gilbert and Sullivan's *Trial by Jury* — one of the most perfect works they ever wrote. In between, a *pas de deux* from Offenbach's ballet *Le Papillon* was danced by Lois Strike and Kelvin Coe. Christopher Renshaw (producer) and Kenneth Rowell (designer) created a very amusing theatrical evening and the splendid cast enjoyed themselves, as did the public. 'The whole team, almost fifty strong, contains nothing but winners,' wrote Fred Blanks in *The Sydney Morning Herald*, and Elizabeth Swallow had this to say in *The Daily Telegraph*:

> 'The Australian Opera shrugged off its restraint and dived into an operatic custard pie with its productions of *Trial by Jury* and *Ba-ta-clan*. And after the performance, which would have left Gilbert, Offenbach and Sullivan giggling in their graves, there was hardly a straight face left in the Opera House. For this little show *An Evening with Gilbert, Offenbach and Sullivan* is a real charmer.'

Above: The Dialogues of the Carmelites
Joan Sutherland as Madame Lidoine in
the Prison Scene

In *Trial by Jury* Gordon Wilcock looking like Humpty-Dumpty, played the Judge, Anthony Warlow — the Defendant, Anne-Maree McDonald — the Plaintiff, John Fulford — the Counsel for the Plaintiff, and John Germain — the Usher, and very good they all were.

Ba-ta-clan had the same cast as before, although Michael Smith went on as Ké-ki-ka-ko in one of the performances for the indisposed Paul Ferris.

During July and August we revived for eight performances *Les Contes d'Hoffmann*, the opera in which we had first appeared with the Company ten years before. The cast this time was all new with the exception of Donald Solomon's Luther, Robert Eddie's Schlemil and Graeme Ewer, who repeated his enchanting performances of Andrès, Cochenille, Pitichinaccio and Frantz — his Frantz being amongst my fondest memories. Jonathan Summers sang the four baritone roles and Horst Hoffmann made his début with the Company as Hoffmann, and has stayed as resident tenor with a wide-ranging repertoire. Bernadette Cullen sang the Muse and Nicklausse, Anthony Warlow — Spalanzani, Pieter van der Stolk — Crespel, and Jeffrey Black and Christopher Dawes were the students.

'Sutherland triumphs in a spellbinding *Hoffmann*,' headlined Maria Prerauer in *The Australian*:

'Dame Joan Sutherland and her conductor husband Richard Bonynge's tenth anniversary performance of Offenbach's *The Tales of Hoffmann* on Friday turned into a personal triumph ... It was almost as though the magic spell that runs through the plot of *The Tales of Hoffmann* had even spilled over into the night itself, making Dame Joan's voice suddenly sound even fresher and more radiantly beautiful, if that were at all possible, than it had ten years earlier.

Her mechanical doll Olympia was, as then, nothing less than phenomenal, vocally

Above: The Marriage of Figaro Michael Lewis as Count Almaviva
Right: The Marriage of Figaro Act 3. (Left to right) Graeme Ewer (Basilio), Michael Lewis (the Count), Rosina Raisbeck (Marcellina) and Pieter van der Stolk (Bartolo)

astonishing in its combination of luscious tone and quicksilver colouratura. And she went through the stiff-armed, glassy-eyed, lash-fluttering spiel of the life-size, wound-up automaton with just the right touch of understated humour. And where most divas are content to tackle only one of Hoffmann's four disastrous loves, Dame Joan again sang all the others as well … the heartless Venetian Contessa Giulietta … the poor little consumptive, Antonia, and the imperious opera singer, Stella. It was a tour-de-force worthy of such a special occasion.'

W.L. Hoffman of *The Canberra Times* wrote:

'The sheer brilliance and magic of the sound in Olympia's aria in the first act was spellbinding. This performance aroused a sustained ovation from the audience, an ovation only surpassed at the end of the wonderful trio which concluded with Antonia's death … Richard Bonynge directed the performance with all the care and style that he brings to the French operatic repertoire … The ovation that Richard Bonynge received when he made his first appearance in the pit, and the warm enthusiasm for Sutherland's singing, demonstrated a personal warmth and affection, and gratitude for the pleasure and many memorable moments that they have brought to opera audiences over the past ten years.'

And *The Catholic Weekly* commented:

'Bonynge once again demonstrates his uncanny ability to get the best possible playing for the opera of the occasion, and here he obtains playing that provides glow and passion.'

On 19 August, Stuart Challender and I shared the conducting in a concert enti-

Above: The Marriage of Figaro (from left to right) John Pringle as Figaro, Glenys Fowles as Susanna, Michael Lewis as the Count and Joan Carden as the Countess

tled 'Musicians for World Peace' presented with the support of the United Nations Association of Australia. Apart from Joan's 'Casta Diva' and the *Lucia* Mad Scene, I remember Paul and Maud Tortellier playing the incredibly difficult Paganini *Variations on one string on a theme of Rossini*. They did this with such panache that it seemed almost like a great music-hall turn — they were wonderful.

Poulenc's *Dialogues of the Carmelites* entered the repertory for the first time in September and this great Catholic masterpiece even survived being conducted by a Protestant and directed by a Jew!

Joan had sung in the first English performances at Covent Garden as Madame Lidoine, the new Prioress, in 1958 when the composer had been in attendance for the rehearsals. It took some persuading to get her to relearn the part but I think she was glad she made the effort. The cast gelled in an extraordinary way and the whole experience was an extremely moving one.

Isobel Buchanan was Blanche, Lone Koppel the old Prioress, Heather Begg — Mère Marie, and Anne-Maree McDonald and Fiona Maconaghie — Soeur Constance. Geoffrey Chard sang the Marquis, Paul Ferris — the Chevalier, Richard Greager — the Priest, John Fulford — the Gaoler, Pieter van der Stolk — the Officer, Gordon Wilcock and John Wegner — the commissaries, Anthony Warlow — Thierry, and John Germain — M. Javelinot. Mère Jeanne was played by Patricia Price, Soeur Mathilde by Cynthia Johnston, and the remaining sisters I must name because each one by their commitment added greatly to the emotional effect of the opera: Frances Chambers, Judith Saliba, Olga Sanderson-Smith, Marie-Thérèse Driscoll, Helen Adams, Beryl Furlan, Luise Napier, Helen Borthwick, Hellen O'Rourke, Deborah Riedel and Dorothy Robertson-O'Brien.

The production (we did nine performances) was by Elijah Moshinsky and the design by John Bury. The whole was televised and released on videotape.

'The Australian Opera's presentation of Poulenc's *Dialogues of the Carmelites*,' wrote Roger Covell:

'does honour to the Company and to the art of opera ... *The Carmelites* is, I think, the newest opera that Richard Bonynge has conducted here. That he does it so well need not surprise us: Poulenc's score adheres to the primary operatic tradition of eloquent voices supported (rather than dictated to) by instruments; and this tradition is one of which Bonynge's sensitivity is exceptional.'

He went on to commend 'the commanding moderation of Sutherland as the second prioress.'

The Australian reported:

'Altogether one of the finest productions The Australian Opera has presented this year, in fact among the best for any year.'

Nadine Amadio in *The Sunday Telegraph:*

'Dame Joan Sutherland added a luxurious vocal sheen to the opera with her account of the second prioress ... The musical direction of Poulenc's brilliant score was superbly realised by Richard Bonynge. Elegant, sympathetic and aware, his performance was memorable.'

Brian Hoad:

'A rare and vintage performance by Joan Sutherland.'

David Gyger:

'... though there were several fine onstage performances, and a masterly directing stint from Elijah Moshinsky, it was Bonynge's baton that brought it all together musically — and meticulously kept it together over its entire run of nine performances.'

Concurrent with the *Dialogues* I conducted four performances of *The Marriage of Figaro* with Joan Carden as the Countess, Glenys Fowles as Susanna and Bernadette Cullen as Cherubino. Michael Lewis sang the Count, John Pringle — Figaro, Graeme Ewer — Basilio, Rosina Raisbeck — Marcellina, Pieter van der Stolk — Bartolo, Fiona Maconaghie — Barbarina, Christopher Dawes — Curzio and Donald Solomon — Antonio. This fine cast made conducting the opera a joy.

The whole Company was saddened by the death in the Winter Season of Geoffrey Arnold, repetiteur, chorus-master and conductor, a much beloved member of the Company. He is greatly missed.

To end on a brighter note though, in the Queen's birthday honours list I was made an Officer in the Order of Australia for my services to music.

Left: Richard Bonynge after park performance of *Lucia di Lammermoor*

12

NINETEEN EIGHTY FIVE

This year was in some ways quite disastrous for the Company, which was torn in all directions. The number of performances (of 23 operas) was increased to 263, which meant a lowering of standards and a massive overload of work for many of the working Company.

Facing Page: I Puritani as Elvira in the Mad Scene

The performances were increased to make money, yet thousands of dollars were spent on more and more people to work in administration, not to mention the luxurious decorating of the Company offices.

Due to the Australia Council breathing down the backs of the Board and the General Manager, it was decided to mount not just one Australian opera but two, plus an evening of three one-act Australian pieces: five works which would probably never be seen again. The strain on the mental and physical health of the singers and *répétiteurs* was enormous and the amount of illness in the company was catastrophic. I remember at least two nights when there were six singers ill, and it was the exception to have a performance with no substitutions. The tragedy was that all the work entailed by these performances was mere lip-service to a bunch of cranks — a very small minority of the opera-going public.

The two full-length operas, *Metamorphosis* by Brian Howard and *The Little Mermaid* by Anne Boyd, were each given five performances in the Recording Hall of the Opera House — a hall which holds less than two hundred people, so that each opera was seen by less than a thousand people — not even one full house for a regular opera. A great deal of money was spent and hardly anyone heard the pieces anyway. The three one-act operas fared even worse — they were heard only twice — by very few people. They may have been good pieces, but few people would ever know.

The performing Company was very upset and actually sent a letter to the newspapers of no confidence in the Board and the Management. Patrick Veitch was soon gone from the opera — over two years before his contract was up. It seemed that he and the Board could not agree on money or policy.

Our year began with *Les Contes d'Hoffmann* in the Park. The Press reported an attendance in excess of 100,000 and the weather was beautiful. Anson Austin sang Hoffmann, Bruce Martin — Lindorf, Gregory Yurisich — Coppelius, Michael Lewis — Dapertutto, Sebastian Swan — Dr Miracle, John Antoniou — Hermann, and the rest of the cast was the same as in last year's revival.

Our first new production was *Norma*. My original intention was to have given the Australian première of Massenet's beautiful *Esclarmonde*. We had a wonderful cast

Right: Don Pasquale Act 3. Rosamund Illing (Norina) and Gregory Yurisich (Don Pasquale)

and the sets and costumes had already been gloriously designed by Kenneth Rowell. However, as Mr Veitch and the Board preferred to spend the money on decorating their offices, this was jettisoned. They wanted Joan to sing more Lucias or Borgias, but she refused.

Because the locale of the performances was to be the Concert Hall, some large scale work was needed and Ken Rowell was asked to design a new *Norma* — but on a shoestring. Superb designer that he is, he managed to create something which gave a good impression of space and allowed the opera to be performed.

Horst Hoffman sang Pollione, Sandra Hahn — Adalgisa, Donald Shanks — Oroveso, Cynthia Johnston — Clotilde, Gregory Tomlinson — Flavio, and Christopher Renshaw directed.

Maria Prerauer:

'The audience loved every bit of it, breaking again and again into sustained applause ...

Above: Don Pasquale from (left to right) Gregory Yurisich, Don Pasquale; Gordon Wilcock, the Notary; Rosamund Illing, Norina; and Michael Lewis, Dr Malatesta

Left: Don Pasquale Act 1. Rosamund Illing as Norina

Right: Joan Sutherland as *Norma.* Act 1

conductor Richard Bonynge, who has a special affinity with this sort of music, was in his top form.'

Brian Hoad:

'Joan Sutherland rose and rose and rose to the occasion, climaxing the final scene with an outburst of fiery temperament seldom if ever seen before. Here was a diva in that stately and imperious mood which brings Kings and commoners to their knees ... it was a rare fusion of vocal and dramatic power which sent shivers up the spine.'

Joan sang seven performances and, owing to a bout of influenza, Christa Leahmann sang the last two, and very well indeed. She was Joan's understudy, was fully prepared and was very well appreciated by the public.

Our next new production was *Don Pasquale*, and the money allotted for the pro-

duction was minimal. But owing to the cleverness of designer, Roger Kirk, it looked romantic and was produced with great humour by Stuart Maunder. Although this was a period of nasty infighting between the Board and the business management in which the Press joined — hurling rumours and backstage gossip — and although this adversely affected the morale of the Company, our singers somehow managed to rise above these rather unpleasant goings on, and the public in no way suffered.

Gregory Yurisich sang the title role, with Rosamund Illing as Norina, Richard Greager — Ernesto, Michael Lewis — Dr Malatesta, and Gordon Wilcock — the Notary.

Wrote Patricia Brown in *The Sydney Morning Herald*:

'Surprisingly for a musician justly famous in the repertoire, the current production of *Don Pasquale* marks Richard Bonynge's conducting début of the opera. From the opening cello solo of the overture, through the complexities of the Act II finale and on to the

Above Top: The Mikado Act 1. (Left to right) Jennifer Bermingham (Pitti-Sing), Anne-Maree McDonald (Peep-Bo), Jennifer McGregor (Yum-Yum), Michael Smith (Nanki-Poo), Gregory Yurisich (Pooh-Bah) and John Germain (Pish-Tush)
Above: The Mikado Heather Begg as Katisha; Graeme Ewer as Ko-Ko
Facing Page: The Mikado from *above:* Bruce Martin as the Mikado and Heather Begg as Katisha. *Below:* Graeme Ewer as Ko-Ko; Jennifer Bermingham as Pitti-Sing and Gregory Yurisich as Pooh-Bah

swift, moral-pointing conclusion, he kept orchestra, soloist and chorus bubbling along with never a dull moment.'

She continued:

(Rosamund Illing's) 'vocal and physical characterisations are unerringly varied and apt. This is a Norina whose energy and musical accuracy strike just the right balance between a resourceful, heartless commedia heroine and a character capable of deeper insights.'

Nadine Amadio:

'Donizetti is Richard Bonynge's home territory and his stylish musical direction was the sparkling driving force behind the performance … The Australian Opera's elegant new production of Donizetti's *Don Pasquale* brings polish and wit to the small operatic gem … (Gregory Yurisich) gives a tour-de-force performance.'

We gave six performances during February and it was repeated for a further eight, with a complete change of cast later in the year.

Our last engagement during the summer was to have been a televised gala from the new Victorian Arts Centre in Melbourne of *Les Contes d'Hoffmann* to open their summer season. There had been a dispute between The Theatrical Management and several of the unions over the travelling allowance to be paid while on tour. I believe the unions were not taken sufficiently seriously and junior executives were sent to negotiate. While frequently in disagreement with union demands, I think it fair to say that, in this instance, they had a case.

Of course, they chose the most glamorous night of the season to make their point. Although the Musicians' Union and Actors Equity were in favour of giving the performance, the Australian Theatrical and Amusement Employees Association was not. The final decision was reached fifty minutes after the curtain was due to go up and the public was sent home.

The Australian Opera had to refund the patrons about $125,000, which it could
ill afford, and the wider Australian public missed out on a rather beautiful production of *The Tales of Hoffmann*. It was not reinstated, as we were obliged to leave for
overseas engagements.

On returning for the winter season we were able to make some recompense as we
brought with us Marilyn Horne and gave a gala opera concert (at gala prices) which
was televised throughout the country. She and Joan sang duos from *Norma*,
Semiramide, *Lakmé*, and several arias each. We first gave the concert in Melbourne
and three days later repeated it in Sydney.

In June a new production of Gilbert and Sullivan's *Mikado* was launched. Gilbert
and Sullivan's musicals are much loved by the Australian public and many performances can be scheduled and numerous revivals assured. I had enjoyed *Trial by Jury*
so much that I was delighted to prepare and conduct the first six performances of the
season's thirty-six. Christopher Renshaw directed, Tim Goodchild designed the
most witty production and several of the cast were old hands at the genre. As the

'three little maids' we had Jennifer McGregor, Jennifer Bermingham and Anne-Maree McDonald. Nanki-Poo was Michael Smith, Ko-ko — Graeme Ewer, Pooh-Bah — Gregory Yurisich, Pish-Tush — John Germain, Katisha — Heather Begg, and the Mikado — Bruce Martin. We had a very jolly time with this very funny and masterly work and I have never seen it better performed.

I was brought up on Gilbert and Sullivan and saw the pieces constantly throughout the forties in Sydney — there was little else to see.

On 24 June we opened a new production of Bellini's *I Puritani* for seven performances. This was produced by Sir Robert Helpmann with sets by Henry Bardon and costumes by Michael Stennett. The whole looked very handsome and Sir Robert magically brought this most romantic of *bel canto* pieces to life.

Anson Austin sang the stratospheric part of Arturo and the higher the part the happier he seemed. Michael Lewis sang Riccardo with very beautiful line and Donald Shanks was entirely sympathetic as Giorgio, the heroine's uncle, and made Elivra seem almost fragile, he dwarfed her so. Rosemary Gunn was the Queen, John Wegner — Lord Walton and Christopher Dawes — Bruno.

W.L. Hoffmann thought Joan's voice had

> 'amazing flexibility, and a tonal splendour and power which enables it to ride out with thrilling effect over the other principals, chorus and orchestra, in the climactic moments of the opera ... Sutherland in a cast, and singing at her best, seems to elicit a high response from every member of the cast, and this is the case here. The chorus, too, sings with character and spirit, and Richard Bonynge conducting the performance with his innate feeling for the spirit of these *bel canto* operas also obtains beautifully expressive playing from the orchestra ... this is a notable presentation of *I Puritani*, with singing which few opera houses in the world could match.'

Above Top: Così Fan Tutte (left to right) Act 1 Finale. Margaret Russell as Dorabella, Joan Carden as Fiordiligi, John Fulford as Guglielmo, Monique Brynnel as Despina and Glen Winslade as Ferrando
Above: Così Fan Tutte Monique Brynnel as Despina

Fred Blanks wrote of her in *The Sydney Morning Herald:*

> 'Intensely-sustained lyricism, punctuated by runs, trills and top notes held with unswerv-

Above: I Puritani Act 1 with Michael Lewis as Riccardo
Right: I Puritani Act 1 with Anson Austin (Arturo)

ing steadiness ... her voice is unquenchable.'

Maria Prerauer:

> 'Sutherland's Elvira is not only magnificently sustained vocally but even histrionically it is possible to believe that she is a pathetic young girl pushed beyond the bounds of reason.'

and Brian Hoad:

> '*I Puritani* is simply a marvellous show-case for the art of the prima donna in which field, at the age of 58, Sutherland still reigns supreme.'

Once again I was fortunate to conclude my work in the season with some Mozart performances. A revival of John Copley's production of *Così fan tutte*, rehearsed by John Wregg, was scheduled to begin on 9 July, and I had hoped to do the first four performances. However, it was my turn to catch the 'flu and I missed the first night. My cover conductor, Andrew Greene, had been released for some work in New Zealand and arrived back too late for the first act but conducted the second. The first was conducted at very short notice by Stuart Challender, who had not conducted the piece for a few years.

Joan Carden was a most musically accomplished Fiordiligi and Margaret Russell, her vivacious sister. Glenn Winslade sang very stylishly as Ferrando, well supported by John Fulford as Guglielmo and Geoffrey Chard as Don Alfonso. Monique

Brynnel who considers herself strictly an operetta singer brought great panache to her first operatic role, Despina. I so enjoyed my three performances and would have liked more.

Although I think this entire season was far too heavy for any Company, it certainly proved what the singers, orchestra, music staff and stage staff could cope with under extreme pressure. But not without some cost. Among the 263 performances noted (which included six weeks of touring), there were performances of simple little pieces like *Elektra* (in concert), *Die Walküre, Jenufa, Katya Kabanova* and *The Dialogues of the Carmelites*, as well as a few Verdi's and Puccini's. Hats off to a very tough Company!

13

NINETEEN EIGHTY SIX

On arrival in Australia in January our first performance was for the Western Australia Opera Company in Perth where we gave an operatic concert with Bernadette Cullen and the Western Australian Arts Orchestra. Bernadette and Joan sang duets from *Norma* and *Semiramide* as well as several arias apiece.

Facing Page: Marie in *La Fille du Régiment* Act 1

This year marked our last Opera in the Park which we had inaugurated in 1982 and performed five years running. The opera was *Rigoletto*, the title role wonderfully sung by Michael Lewis with Richard Greager as the Duke, Donald Shanks as both Monterone and Sparafucile, and Rosemary Gunn as Maddalena. This was Joan's only Gilda in Australia and she had not sung the role since the Verdi Festival at the Metropolitan Opera, New York in 1972.

The *Sydney Sun* called her 'Saint Joan of Sydney' and went on:

> 'Someone recently remarked that she sounds like a young soprano — except that there isn't a young soprano who sounds half as good.'

David Gyger wrote:

> 'She can sing the role stupendously as ever — and proved so beyond doubt on Monday January 20th … the particular personal triumph of the night as I saw it was the conducting of Richard Bonynge, which displayed the right mix of musical passion and dramatic fire required to do full justice to the work in performance.'

David Vance in *The Sydney Morning Herald:*

> 'To witness the immense crowd intent on every note, caught in a mounting drama of the music, suggests that opera remains the most thrilling of all the performing arts.'

The performance was to have been held on the previous Saturday but torrential rains intervened. On the Monday, even with threatening clouds, people began arriving at just after five in the morning to stake out the best spots.

We gave five more *Lucia's* in the Concert Hall and it was simulcast and released on videotape. John Wregg reproduced the Copley production with Richard Greager as Edgardo, Malcolm Donnelly (his début with The Australian Opera) as Enrico, Clifford Grant and John Wegner as Raimondo, Patricia Price — Alisa, Robin

Above Top: Lucia di Lammermoor Act 2
Scene 2. Wedding Scene
Above: Lucia di Lammermoor Mad Scene

Donald — Normanno, and Sergei Baigildin — Arturo. Maria Prerauer described it as 'The stuff of folk legend', and *The Sun Herald* reported that Joan had the greatest standing ovation of any artist in the Opera House's thirteen-year history.

Nadine Amadio wrote:

'She sang with effortless beauty through those dazzling vocal gymnastics. It is almost a quarter of a century since that historic night in Covent Garden when Sutherland sang her first Lucia and a legend was born. It seems that her voice has lost little of its freshness or beauty. What has been added is depth of experience, absolute professionalism and a moving insight into the music of this role.'

And from Ron Roberts in *The Catholic Weekly*:

'Once again, Dame Joan is quite unforgettable, being a great voice and still possessor of that magnetism that makes all she does so compelling. Her vocal resources seem to have no limits and stemming from that she attacks the part of Lucia as though realising the character's potential for the first time, refining all pertinent aspects of it. Her trills and the decoration of certain high notes are not emphatically stressed, but retain their brilliant quality. Added to this, her voice has a warmer glow to it than of yore. Her "Mad Scene" has metamorphosed. No longer a thing of dramatic hysteria, it now builds slowly to a gentle nightmare with no element of an exercise in virtuosity embedded in it. This is both singing and characterisation of great quality.'

A new production of *The Magic Flute* was added to the repertory in February. I conducted five performances then, and a further seven in July/August. Perhaps it was sentimentality on my part that I missed the old Copley production, which had given me immense pleasure and was the first opera I had conducted as Musical Director of the Company. I found this new one rather stark, cold and unmagical. I confess, however, that when I watched our video which was released towards the end of the year, I enjoyed it much more.

The new *Flute* was directed by Göran Järvefelt and designed by Carl Friedrich Oberle. Pamina was sung very beautifully by both Amanda Thane and Yvonne

Left: Lucia di Lammermoor Act 1
Scene 2

Above: The Magic Flute Christa
Leahmann as the Queen of the Night
Above Centre: The Magic Flute Act 1
Gran Wilson as Tamino
Above Right: The Magic Flute Act 1
Hakan Hagagard as Papageno
Right: The Magic Flute The three genii

Kenny, and Gran Wilson sang all the Taminos. There were three Papagenos —
Hakan Hagegaard (in February) Jeffrey Black and John Fulford. The latter stepped
in at the last moment, without rehearsal, for an indisposed Black at the television
performance and his professionalism may be gauged by the videotape. Christa
Leahmann once again gave her startling performance as the Queen of the Night
with Donald Shanks in his old role of Sarastro. The Three Ladies were sung by
Rosamund Illing/Nicola Waite, Bernadette Cullen/Patricia Price and Rosemary
Gunn. The boys were endearingly performed by Andrew Phipps, Andrew Wentzel
and Cameron Phipps. The director insisted that Graeme Ewer play Monostatos with
deadly seriousness, contrasting with the former production's lighter and more comic
view of the character. The words that Monostatos speaks are appalling if taken
absolutely seriously but Mozart wrote for the character light and charming music
with no note of the sinister. Graeme made me laugh anyway (sorry Graeme!). The
Speaker was treble-cast with Arend Baumann, John Pringle and Stephen Bennett, a
Priest was sung by Robin Donald, the Armed Men by Sergei Baigildin and Joseph
Grunfelder, and Papagena by Peta Blyth.

Above Top: La Fille du Régiment The
music lesson scene, with Heather Begg
as the Marquise
Above: La Fille du Régiment Act 1 Anson
Austin as Tonio

Brian Hoad had this to say:

> 'The orchestra under the baton of Richard Bonynge illuminates the stage and the stage
> illuminates the music to present a sublime work of art through which we can all measure
> our humanity.'

After three concerts for the Wellington Festival in New Zealand in early March
we returned to Europe.
We were back in July for a new production of *La Fille du Régiment*, and a charming

Above Top: La Fille du Régiment Act 1.
(Left to right) Gregory Yurisich
(Sulpice), Joan Sutherland (Marie) and
Anson Austin (Tonio)
Above: Marie in *La Fille du Régiment*
Act 2

one it was. Sandro Sequi came to produce it — we had worked together on the same opera in Covent Garden, the Met, Chicago, and Vancouver. The sets were by Henry Bardon and the costumes by Michael Stennett. Anson Austin sang Tonio, Gregory Yurisich — Sulpice and Heather Begg the Marquise. Gordon Wilcock was Hortensius, Marie-Claire — the Duchess, David Lemke — the Corporal and Stephen Bennett — a Peasant.

Brian Hoad was complimentary:

> 'It is the 18th production which Sutherland has starred in for this Company — and the happiest. ...the music bubbles along irrepressibly under the baton of Richard Bonynge through a marvellous mix of solos and duets and ensembles and jolly drunken soldiers songs, of humour, sentiment and wit. Sutherland in brilliant voice and high spirits, switched effortlessly from broad comedy to touching pathos ... A good time was had by all — all except the snobs.'

The 'local prince of the high C's' he called Anson Austin, and rightly so — of the D flat's one might also add.

Maria Prerauer wrote:

> 'Dame Joan Sutherland has made the cute heroine Marie, the regimental teenage mascot, as much her own as the tragic Lucia. The only surprise is that The Australian Opera took so long to mount a production for her.

Tuesday's first night was, of course, a great personal success. Sutherland tossed off the soprano's florid runs and trills like a lark ascending while romping round the stage with the tongue-in-cheek nonchalance of a born comedian.'

Above: La Fille du Régiment Act 1

And Roger Covell:

'No experience in 1986 has been quite like attending a performance of The Australian Opera's *Daughter of the Regiment*, with Dame Joan Sutherland in the title role ... I can only describe it as a process of complete communication and sympathy between performer and audience ... the truly memorable part of the occasion was the audience's relationship with Sutherland. It is an expression of absolute trust in and total commitment of the personality and gifts of the performer ... Sutherland held the audience with her unusually good comedienne's craft and the unaffected charm of her stage presence. I was put in mind of the legends of Nellie Stewart and Gladys Moncrieff at their best. She has managed to establish a relationship with the Australian public which bears comparison with the musical comedy queens of a former age as well as, of course, earning an inter-

Above: La Fille du Régiment Marie-Claire
as the Duchess of Crackenthorp

national operatic reputation at the highest level. That is a rare, probably an unrepeatable combination. It deserves notice.'

This made a wonderful end for us to the 1986 season. However, after we left the country there was a deal of unrest. The singers called for the resignation of Patrick Veitch and Charles Berg, the Chairman of the Board. Charles Berg resigned — but one must remember with gratitude that he gave voluntarily and unselfishly of his time and effort for many years to The Australian Opera. He died the following year.
The Sydney Morning Herald of 16 October reported:

'Meetings of staff from The Australian Opera have been called for today in order to announce the departure of the Company's General Manager, Mr Patrick Veitch.
The announcement will bring to an end a long period of controversy within the Company, whose singers called for Mr Veitch's resignation in February this year.'

Veitch's contract had been due to expire at the end of 1988.

Above: After a concert at the
Wellington Festival

14
NINETEEN EIGHTY EIGHT
TO NINETY

After eleven consecutive years of performing with The Australian Opera, it did us, and I daresay our public, some good to spend a year apart. We had done all we were capable of with willingness and pleasure, and had ourselves received great emotional rewards.

Facing Page: The Merry Widow waltz Act 3

The Company sent me a contract to return with the title of Musical Director Emeritus and Principal Guest Conductor. I appreciated this gesture of goodwill but refused, not because my feelings for the Company had changed, but because I wanted to be quite free of any ties.

This proved to be the right decision. On returning in 1988 the slightly uncomfortable boss-employee relationship had vanished and I relaxed and enjoyed myself more than ever before — I had always felt among friends with the Company but now I was just one of them.

While away we were sad to hear of the death of Peter Seymour, who had worked with us as conductor, chorus master and administrator for almost ten years. He was the kindest and most encouraging of men. He made a great contribution to the musical life of Sydney, not only in the Opera House but also with The Sydney Philharmonia Society, whose Musical Director he had been since 1969 and with whom he introduced to the public much unknown music of three centuries.

For this bicentenary year of our country, which was after all a celebration, we decided to return with *The Merry Widow*. I conducted fifteen performances with three Widows. Lovely Glenys Fowles sang seven, young Christine Douglas sang two when Glenys was indisposed and surprised us very pleasurably with a great deal of stage know-how, and Joan sang six.

Joan's performances were turned into galas with seats at the highest price ever charged for an opera in Australia — $150 top — which she found slightly embarrassing. However, she was glad to help swell the Opera's ever-needing coffers. Of course, at these prices, excitement was higher than ever and much was expected.

Stuart Maunder did a wonderful job reviving the Mansouri production and the cast was full of old friends and a couple of new ones. Ronald Stevens was Danilo, Anson Austin — Camille, Anne-Maree McDonald — Valencienne, Gordon Wilcock — Baron Zeta, Graeme Ewer — Njegus, and Jennifer Bermingham — Zozo. Christopher Dawes was St Brioche, Neil Kirkby — Cascada, John Germain — Kromow, Donald Solomon — Pritschitch, David Brennan — Bogdanovich and Jonathon Welch — the Maitre d'Hotel. Rosina Raisbeck was Praskovia; Caroline

Above Top: The Merry Widow Act 3 with Ronald Stevens as Danilo
Above: The Merry Widow Act 1 with Ronald Stevens as Danilo

Clack, Sylviane, and Irenie Cassimitas, Olga. The ballet, led by Lois Strike who has danced in so many ballets with the Company for many years, seemed more splendid than before.

Nadine Amadio summed up Joan's performances nicely:

> 'That she has a dazzling on-stage charisma is not so surprising when one considers her legendary career … What we have now is a *grande dame* of the stage with a warm and glowing voice, a true musician, a great professional with glamour and a magnificent presence.
>
> Bonynge has made high class operetta one of his specialities. He brings to it all the style and pizzaz and tongue-in-cheek fun that turns *The Merry Widow* into stage champagne.'

One of the performances was televised, beautifully directed by Virginia Lumsden and is due for release as a video cassette.

On 19 February Joan and I gave a recital in the Ballroom of the newly restored Queen Victoria Building, in Sydney, in aid of The Children's Hospital. At the end of the evening Mr James Fairfax presented Dr John Yu, the General Superintendent of the Hospital, with his personal cheque for one million dollars!

I took part in a concert organised by Michael Lewis and his wife, Patricia Price, at the Willoughby Town Hall, which they charmingly called 'A Gala Concert with Richard Bonynge and Friend's. Sharolyn Kimmorley, David Stanhope and I accompanied the singers and also managed a few four-handed and even six-handed operatic arrangements, with a lot of wrong notes from yours truly who doesn't do much piano-practice these days. Along with Michael and Patricia, Suzanne Johnston, Bernadette Cullen, Jan Saint-John, Amanda Thane, Anson Austin, Kenneth Collins, Donald Shanks and John Fulford, all gave their services and raised money for the music programme at Warrawee School, where the Lewis boys are being educated. I think the audience had as much fun as we did.

I returned in July to conduct five performances of *Fra Diavolo*. I am happy that the public still enjoys this sparkling little piece, which was first in the repertory back in 1977.

Wrote Roger Covell:

> 'The work is a durable and exceptionally tuneful example of French opéra-comique in the hedonistic manner of the earlier part of the nineteenth century.
>
> Auber's touch is light and his craftsmanship thorough … Richard Bonynge understands the pace of the score very well. Although there are times when he seems over-addicted to a fortissimo glare in dynamics, the essential spirit of the music comes across persuasively in instrumental and vocal terms.'

This year the cast had Jennifer McGregor as an enchanting Zerlina, Anson Austin and Paul Ferris repeated their roles of Diavolo and Lorenzo with Heather Begg and Gordon Wilcock as Lord and Lady Allcash, ever an outrageous duo. Graeme Ewer and Stephen Bennett played Beppo and Giacomo, Clifford Grant was the Innkeeper and Geoffrey Crook, the Peasant. This little piece retains its freshness and we all enjoyed the light-hearted romp.

Towards the end of my visit I judged (along with Margreta Elkins and Robert Allman) the Pan-Pacific finalists of the Metropolitan Opera Auditions, and the winner was tenor Jeffrey Ward. The same boy had previously won the Bond Tenor Scholarship for this year. Another tenor, David Hobson, won the Joan Sutherland Scholarship, awarded by Sheila Prior's Australian Opera Auditions Committee, so

perhaps the drought of tenors is beginning to end, at least in Australia. David has already had considerable success in *Fiddler on the Roof*, *The Gondoliers*, *Il Barbiere di Siviglia* and *Così fan tutte*.

This season was for Joan and myself a real relaxation. It was great to return and find the Company calm and happy. The new General Manager, Donald McDonald, obviously cares about the Company and is a calm, non-aggressive man. He and my old friend Moffatt (not so old of course, he's just been there forever) manage to keep things on an even keel. It is a Company that I am proud to have been part of and with which I am proud to continue my association.

In August 1989 The Australian Opera mounted a new production of Bizet's *Le Pêcheurs de Perles*. A poll had been taken among opera goers in Victoria and New South Wales to ascertain what opera the public would like added to the repertoire. The surprising answer was Bizet's youthful and melodious work, which had not been heard in Sydney or Melbourne for about ten years.

A relaxed and enjoyable month was spent rehearsing — it hardly seemed like work. Amanda Thane sang Leila, fulfilling all her early promise and bringing exquisite femininity and warmth to the role. Anson Austin successfully added Nadir to his long list of roles which includes the most difficult in the repertoire and Michael Lewis gave us a splendidly sung and intense Zurga. Clifford Grant missed the first three performances of Nourabad due to the 'flu virus which hit Sydney — the same virus knocked out thirteen members of the chorus at one performance! John Wegner replaced Cliff, who returned for the next five.

Above: The Merry Widow Act 1 (Right to left) Neil Kirkby as Cascada, Christopher Dawes as St Brioche, Donald Solomon as Pritschitch, Gordon Wilcock as Baron Zeta, John Germain as Kromow and David Brennan as Bogdanovitch

Above: Amanda Thane as Leila in *Les Pêcheurs de Perles*

Lindy Hume who had come up through the ranks as a dancer in many of our productions made her directorial début with The Australian Opera and it was a pleasure to work with her. Kenneth Rowell designed the romantic production.

On returning to Australia in March 1990 I found the Company in a state of shock. The tragic death of John Fulford at only 43 saddened us all — he was much loved both as friend and artist.

I worked with him for many years from his beginnings in small roles to his mastery of major ones. His Papageno and Guglielmo had great humanity — he showed a delicious sense of humour in *Trial by Jury* and a reserve of power as Enrico in *Lucia di Lammermoor.* His performances of the latter in the parks with Joan in 1984 was a highlight of his career. How fortunate we are to have a souvenir of his Papageno preserved on videotape.

As this book is about to go to press we have just finished twelve performances of Emmerich Kalmán's *The Gipsy Princess* in Melbourne. Nigel Douglas who has had a world of experience with operetta on both sides of the footlights directed and the cast reacted to him enthusiastically. The amusing and musical choreography is by Michèle Hardy, another very welcome newcomer to Australia.

Kenneth Rowell has designed glamorous sets and Victoria Rowell has hand-painted the exquisite 1915 costumes. Deborah Riedel plays the diva of Hungarian cabaret — Sylva Varescu. She began in our chorus some years ago as a mezzo-soprano and has developed into a gorgeous lyric soprano with a very wide range and even production throughout. Roxane Hislop is an enchanting Stasi, an ornament to the stage. Roger Lemke shows great comedic flair and splendid voice as Count Boni.

I am working with these three singers for the first time, and if they are any example, opera in Australia is in a healthy state.

The rest of the cast are old friends — Anson Austin as Prince Edwin, Graeme Ewer as Baron Feri, Heather Begg and Robert Gard as the Prince and Princess Von and Zu Lippert-Weilersheim. Gordon Wilcock doubles as the lawyer Kisch and the porter, Neil Kirkby plays Baron von Rohnsdorff and Geoffrey Crook the American Ambassador. Judith Henley, Jonathan Welch and Paul Ferris perform in Sydney.

The ballet girls are delicious and the eight of the chorus men who execute some pretty difficult routines, do so with panache. Joe Grunfelder dances the Viennese waltz as to the manner born.

The Melbourne public at the première was warm and generous in its laughter and applause. The composer's daughter Yvonne came for the opening and looked very happy.

I am scheduled to conduct twenty-six performances throughout the year and there are thirty-seven in all, with colleague Neil Flottman conducting the remaining eleven.

All being well, Joan will return to sing her farewell to grand opera and to her Australian public in September in *Les Huguenots* — eight are scheduled with a grand gala finale on 2 October.

I know she is loved by the Australian public and it is a mutual love affair.

Recently, Jenny Stevens of *The Sun Herald* was writing an article about Joan and interviewed her dresser of long-standing at the opera, Sandy, who said very endearingly: 'There is Joan Sutherland, the Queen and God — it's that simple.'

'A slight exaggeration' said the Dame, but was touched none the less.

As to the future — who knows? I look forward to revivals of *Carmen* and *Roméo et Juliette* in the next two years as well as a new production of Donizetti's *Maria Stuarda* — another first for the Australian Opera.

I look back over the past fifteen years with pleasure and see many changes in the

Above: Curtain call after the last night of the *Widow*

Australian operatic scene. It is satisfying to see revivals of so many pieces I intro-
duced into the repertoire — *Alcina, Manon, Lucia di Lammermoor, Roméo et Juliette,
Lucrezia Borgia, I Masnadieri, Fra Diavolo, La Fille du Régiment,* and *Les Huguenots.
I Puritani* which we first did in 1985 has just been loaned to the Victorian State
Opera.

How heartening it was to see Massenet's *Werther* introduced to Australia last year
and so beautifully sung by Bernadette Cullen and Neil Rosenshein.

It has been good watching the development of so many young singers, many of
whom started in the chorus or in the Young Artists Programme — Anthony Warlow
(about to create the title role in *Phantom of the Opera*), Bernadette Cullen, Gregory
Yurisich, Anne-Maree McDonald, Amanda Thane, Gregory Tomlinson, Sandra
Hahn, Stephen Bennett, Nicola Ferner-Waite, David Hobson, David Lemke,
Jonathan Welch and many others. I think their growth has been helped because
they are part of a stable Company.

Opera in Australia is healthy. The public is knowledgeable, generous and adventurous, but they expect a good product.

The Australia Opera is giving them just that. Long may it flourish!

Performers in *The Gypsy Princess*
(left to right): Anson Austin, Deborah
Riedel, Robert Gard, Roxanne Hislop,
Heather Begg, Roger Lemke and
Graeme Ewer

OUR OPERATIC PERFORMANCES IN AUSTRALIA AND NEW ZEALAND 1965 – 1990

* Where not indicated, performances took place in Sydney.

1965
Lucia di Lammermoor
(Joan Sutherland)
Semiramide (Joan Sutherland)
Faust (Joan Sutherland)
La Traviata (Joan Sutherland)
La Sonnambula (Joan Sutherland)
All of these in Melbourne and
    Sydney. Only *La Traviata and
    Lucia di Lammermoor* in Brisbane.
*La Traviata, Lucia di Lammermoor
    and Faust* in Adelaide.

1974
Les Contes d'Hoffmann
    (Joan Sutherland)

1976
The Magic Flute
Lakmé (Joan Sutherland)
Carmen
The Marriage of Figaro
Rigoletto Wellington, New Zealand

1977
Lakmé
Carmen Sydney and Brisbane
Lucrezia Borgia (Joan Sutherland)
The Barber of Seville
Fra Diavolo
Pagliacci
Suor Angelica (Joan Sutherland)

1978
The Merry Widow (Joan Sutherland)
Nabucco Sydney, Adelaide and
    Melbourne
The Marriage of Figaro
Norma (Joan Sutherland)
Don Giovanni
La Traviata

1979
The Merry Widow (Joan Sutherland)
    Sydney, Adelaide and Melbourne
Don Giovanni (Joan Sutherland)
    Melbourne
La Traviata (Joan Sutherland)
    Melbourne and Sydney
    (unscheduled)

Norma (Joan Sutherland) Brisbane
Idomeneo (Joan Sutherland)
Die Entführung aus dem Serail
The Queen of Spades Sydney,
    Adelaide and Melbourne

1980
Lucia di Lammermoor (Joan
    Sutherland) Sydney and Adelaide
The Magic Flute
I Masnadieri (Joan Sutherland)
Rigoletto Sydney and Melbourne
Fra Diavolo

1981
Otello (Joan Sutherland/Cillario)
The Beggar's Opera Sydney and
    Melbourne
La Traviata (Joan Sutherland)
Alcina
Les Huguenots (Joan Sutherland)
Rigoletto
La Buona Figliuola

1982
La Traviata (Joan Sutherland)
    Domain*
Rosina/Ba-ta-clan
Lucrezia Borgia (Joan Sutherland)
Norma
Hamlet
Die Fledermaus (Joan Sutherland)
Manon

1983
Die Fledermaus (Joan Sutherland)
    Domain* and Sydney Opera House
Roméo et Juliette
Alcina (Joan Sutherland)
Lucia di Lammermoor
Il Trovatore (Joan Sutherland)
Il Barbiere di Siviglia
Semiramide (Joan Sutherland)

1984
The Magic Flute
Lucia di Lammermoor
    (Joan Sutherland) Domain*
Adriana Lecouvreur
    (Joan Sutherland)

The Merry Widow
Trial by Jury/Ba-ta-clan
Les Contes d'Hoffman
    (Joan Sutherland)
The Dialogues of the Carmelites
    (Joan Sutherland)
The Marriage of Figaro

1985
Les Contes d'Hoffman
    (Joan Sutherland) Domain*
Norma (Joan Sutherland)
Don Pasquale
The Mikado
I Puritani (Joan Sutherland)
Cosi fan Tutte

1986
Rigoletto (Joan Sutherland) Domain*
Lucia di Lammermoor
    (Joan Sutherland)
The Magic Flute
La Fille du Régiment
    (Joan Sutherland)

1988
The Merry Widow (Joan Sutherland)
Fra Diavolo

1989
Les Pecheurs de Perles

1990
The Gipsy Princess Melbourne and
    Sydney
Les Huguenots (Joan Sutherland)

PICTURE CREDITS

I have tried wherever possible to acknowledge the photgraphers whose pictures I have used in this book.

In this case of the black and white photographs, this was fairly easy as many were stamped on the back; but in the case of colour (mostly taken from unmarked slides), this was often impossible. The photographers in this book bring the operas to life far more than any written word, and I would to thank all those who have helped recall and perpetuate these performances.

I am especially grateful to Branco Gaica, the official photographer to the Australian Opera, whose work I have used profusely.

The Age p. 2; Allan Studios, Collingwood, Victoria pp. 4, 5 (above), 6, 7 (left), 8, 11; Australian Opera pp. 18 (below), 24–5, 28, 35–6; Collection of Heather Begg p. 40; Chester Carone p. 62; Collection of Decca Record Company Limited p. 3 (left); Branco Gaica pp. 48 (below), 49–50, 51 (right), 53, 56 (left), 59–60, 61 (below), 68, 70, 76–7, 82, 84 (upper and lower left), 85 (below), 86–7, 90, 92, 94 (below), 95–7, 98 (left), 99–104, 108, 110–3, 115–7, 119–21, 124, 126 (upper and lower left), 127 (upper left and right), 128 (right), 129 (below), 130 (below), 131, 132 (right), 134 (right), 135–6, 139, 142, 143 (below), 144–6, 148–9, 154 (above), 155, 157, 162, 164–5, 167; Jocelyn Corlin p.161; Barry Glass p. 1; Robert Hartman p. 39; Don McMurdo pp. 23, 48 (above), 52, 61 (above), 63–4, 71–3, 83, 85 (above), 88, 94 (above), 98 (right), 118 (right), 122, 132 (upper left), 134 (left), 137, 140, 143 (above), 150 (right), 151–2, 158 (above), 159–60; Collection of Spiro Malas pp. 7 (right), 10 (left); Collection of Sister·Marie Bernarde pp. 20, 27, 34; Bill Moseley pp. 38, 41; Paul Richardson pp. 127 (below), 128 (upper and lower left), 129 (above), 132 (lower left), 133, 147, 150 (left), 154 (below), 156 (centre, right and below); John Walsh, Sydney p. 18 (above); *Women's Weekly* p. 54; Collection of Dame Joan Sutherland and Richard Bonynge pp. 3 (above), 5 (below), 9–10, 11 (below), 12 (left and right), 13, 14 (left and right), 15–6, 19, 30, 32 (left and right), 33 (left and right), 37, 42–7, 51 (left), 56–8, 65–6, 74, 78–80, 84 (right), 89, 105–6, 109, 114, 118 (left), 125, 126 (right), 130 (above).

INDEX OF ARTISTS

INDEX OF OPERAS IN THE AUSTRALIAN REPERTOIRE OF JOAN SUTHERLAND AND RICHARD BONYNGE